Life Is More Important Than Art

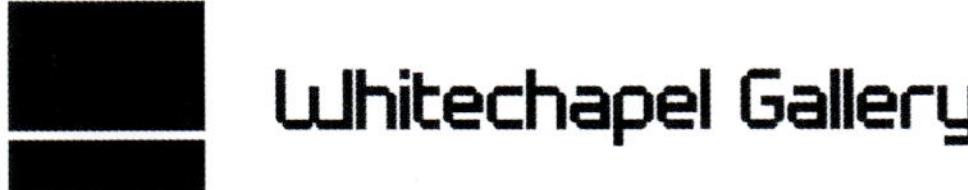

Contents

Foreword

Gilane Tawadros

Life is More Important Than Art (14 June–17 September 2023) is a summer-long, multidisciplinary programme of exhibitions, installations, participatory projects and live events. It explores the intersection of art and everyday life and the role of the contemporary art institution at a time of uncertainty and change. For the first time, the programme occupies all spaces across the Whitechapel Gallery at the same time. The title of the season takes inspiration from African-American writer and novelist James Baldwin, who proposed that life is more important than art … that is why art is important. At a time when the cost of living crisis is causing severe financial hardship and the after-effects of the pandemic are still being felt, we consider the role of art and the art institution in everyday life. What importance can we attach to art alongside more pressing concerns? Representative of, and animated by, the distinctive and radical history of Whitechapel Gallery, *Life is More Important Than Art* points to the critical role that art can play in both reflecting lived experience and opening up new possibilities for thinking, feeling and dreaming.

The exhibition in Galleries 1, 8 and 9, co-curated by Gilane Tawadros and Janette Parris with Katrina Schwarz, maps dynamic histories of migration and difference, with a focus on London and the East End. In the work of twelve artists – Rana Begum, William Cobbing, Sarah Dobai, Susan Hiller, Matthew Krishanu, Jerome, Janette Parris, John Smith, Alia Syed, Mitra Tabrizian, Mark Wallinger and Osman Yousefzada – spanning sculpture, photography, film and installation – past and present histories are interwoven and personal stories are entangled with global events.

The Archive gallery is transformed into *The Somali Museum* by Numbi Arts, a Somali-originated African-centred arts and heritage organisation based in East London. Building on a decades' long friendship with Whitechapel Gallery, *The Somali Museum* imagines how Somali heritage can be celebrated in the UK, with displays that evolve throughout the season. In Gallery 7, artists and play specialists Sarah Marsh and Stephanie Jefferies invite families, school children and audiences of all ages to engage with tactile, sensory objects in *Sculpting Conversations*. In the adjacent gallery, Youth Collective Duchamp & Sons have worked with artist Gaby Sahhar to present *Escape the Slick*, a space to relax, meet friends and reflect on our changing urban landscape.

Broadcast live from Zilkha Auditorium & Studio each week, Whitechapel Gallery Radio Station launches for the summer with artist interviews pegged to the events programme, playlists and more – available to watch live or tune in via the website.

On evenings and weekends, Whitechapel Gallery becomes a fluid space for live talks, performances and takeovers – combining film, food and music, and bringing together contributors from across creative disciplines to discuss pressing issues such as housing, health and migration. Highlight event partners and contributors include Bow Arts, Healing Justice London, Oitij-jo, and our 2023 Writer-in-Residence, Martin O'Brien.

During the daytime, visitors can view Susan Hiller's moving *The J. Street Project (Film)*, 2002–2005 in the former Whitechapel Library, known locally as the 'university of the ghetto'. In Berlin, on an artist's residency, Hiller was startled to encounter a street sign bearing the name *Judenstrasse* (Jews' Street). Intended to commemorate the Jewish community that had once inhabited the area, it also marked a history of discrimination and violent displacement. Over the next three years, Hiller mapped every German street, lane, alley and avenue with the prefix 'Juden' in its name. As the artist writes: 'A photographic image can only, ever, represent things as they are in the present moment when the image is taken'. But the present is a summation of everything that precedes it and each photograph will be seen in the context of everything that happens afterwards. In that way, *The J. Street Project* has allowed me to reflect not only on one unique, incurable, traumatic absence, but also on more recent attempts to destroy minority cultures and erase their presence.'

Led by Director Gilane Tawadros with artist Janette Parris, the summer season's programme project team comprises Richard Martin, Director of Education and Public Programmes, Katrina Schwarz, Curator: Special Projects, Alejandro Ball, Gallery Technical Manager, Eugene Yiu Nam Cheung, Asymmetry Curatorial Fellow, Jane Scarth, Curator: Public Programmes, Siobhán Forshaw, Curator: Community Programmes, Helen Davison, Curator: Family Programmes, Kirsty Lowry, Curator: Schools and Teachers, Luke Gregory-Jones, Head of Visitor Services & Civic Engagement with Sam Williams, Technical Production Manager.

The season is generously supported by:
Sir Frank Bowling
Aldgate Connect BID
The City of London Corporation
ZVM Rangoonwala Foundation
And the Life Is More Important Than Art Exhibition Circle

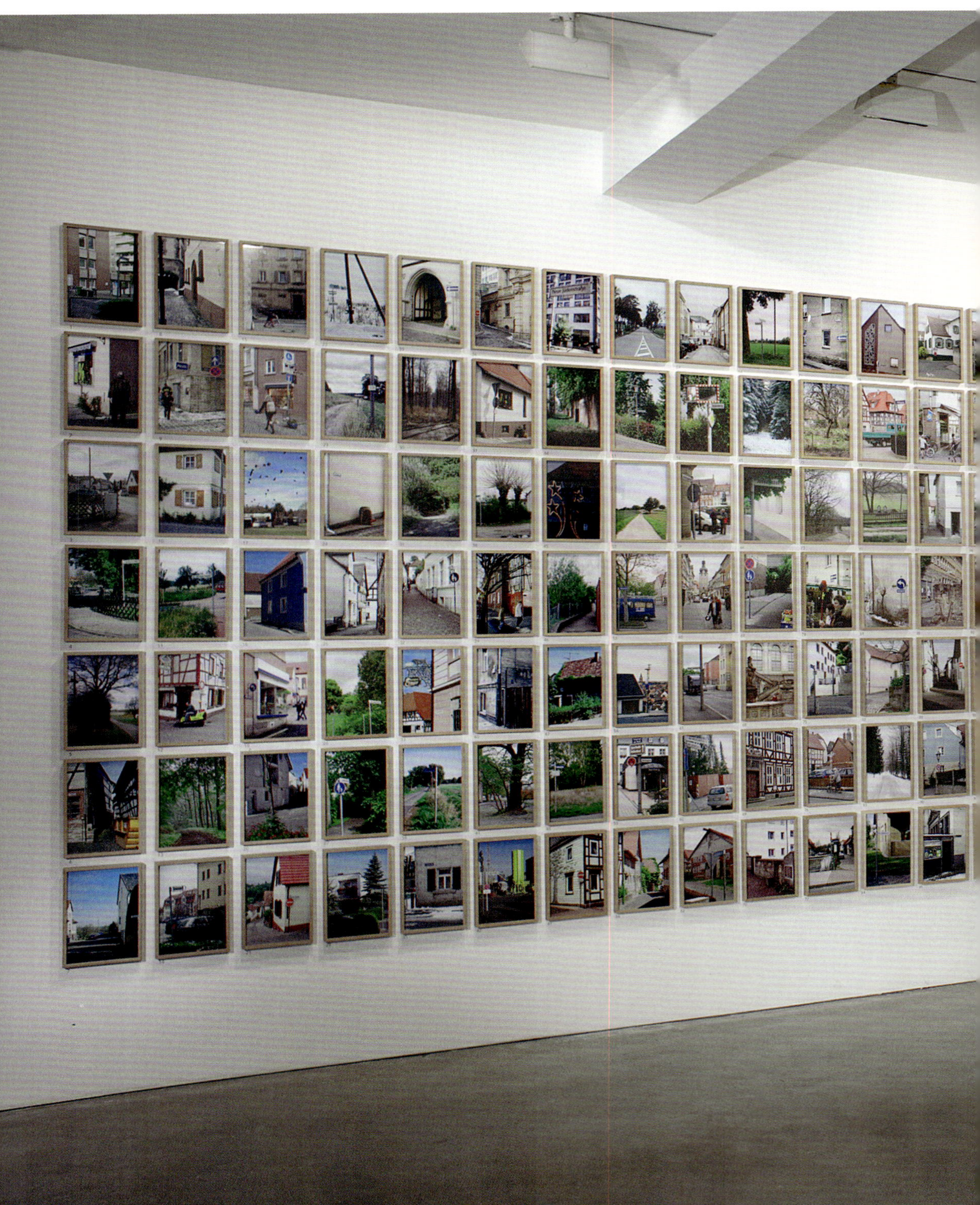

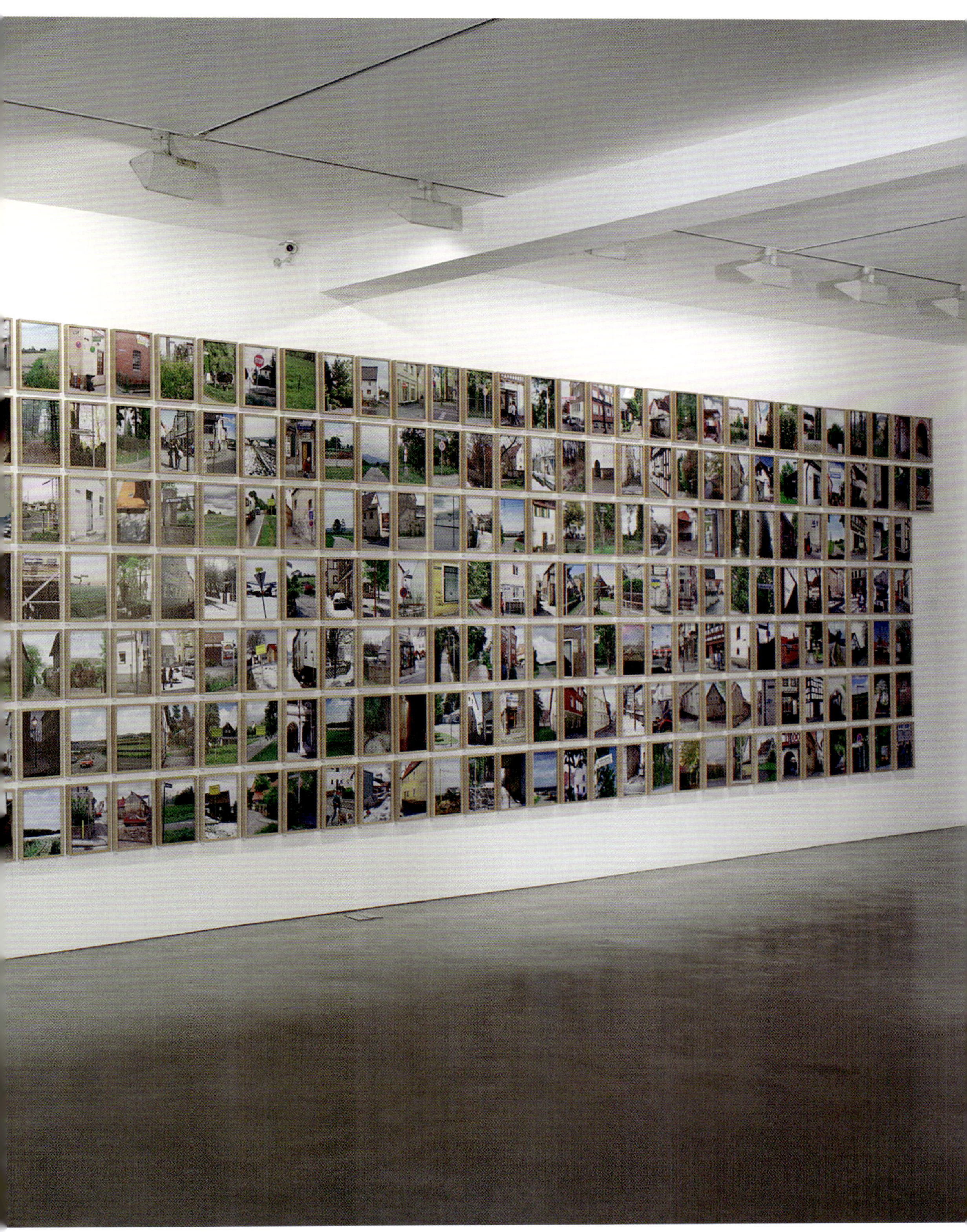

'London is never London...'

Gilane Tawadros and Janette Parris

An old, wooden pushcart is stacked with parcels of various shapes and sizes, individually wrapped in brown paper, tape and string. Each parcel carries a handwritten cardboard label, meticulously detailing its contents. At intervals, the mournful voice of a man singing rises from the stack. Over and again, cantor Josef Rosenblatt ritualistically sings a fragment of the Jewish morning prayer thanking God for restoring the soul after sleep. Retrieved from the muddy gutter of a street in London's East End by the artist Susan Hiller, the parcels contain items apparently discarded during demolition of a building that once housed a tiny shop-front synagogue. As with other of Susan Hiller's works, *Untitled,* 1999, re-claims what has been overlooked and relegated to the periphery: 'Three of the [packages] are remnants of ritual objects [...] ... the fourth is a large ledger from the synagogue's defunct burial society into which I've inserted an old monograph about the numerous 'small synagogues' that once served London's Jewish community [...] the truthfulness of the labels of the wrapped parcels and their significance has to be taken on faith, because what's inside, like the soul, isn't visible'.[1] Poised as if in transit from one place to another, it is unclear whether these parcels are destined for any particular location. No destination has been marked on the luggage labels. These abandoned sacred objects, whose owners have disappeared from view, uncomfortably recall the repeated, violent expulsions and displacements that originally brought those Jewish communities as migrants to the East End of London.

A Pakistani migrant woman's arrival to a new life underpins Osman Yousefzada's installation *An Immigrant's Room of Her Own*, 2018. In a recreation of his mother's bedroom which the artist has described as a migrant version of Virginia Woolf's *A Room of One's Own*, household furniture, cooking pots and personal possessions have been wrapped up in cloth and plastic. Perhaps these objects are being kept purposefully pristine and unused or are in a state of readiness in case their owner needs to gather up their belongings and relocate once again at short notice. Yousefzada's installation speaks to the provisional conditions of many migrants either on account of their political or financial precarity or their anticipation of eventually being able to return 'home' at an unspecified point in the future: 'You take these things into your new life but you don't end up living your new life, that's the contradiction'.[2] Storytelling lies at the heart of Yousefzada's practice, both his art and his writings (and in particular his 2022 memoir *The Go-Between*), which mine his personal history as the child of Pashtun immigrants to Birmingham to articulate the ambiguous and elusive after-effects of migration and displacement: 'No. 12 Willows Road was our house, with its holy green door. Down here on earth the doors of the faithful were always painted green, signifying the colour of the pure, the colour of Islam. We straddled the boundary of Balsall Heath and Moseley. It was on this street and those around it that all the immigrants – Black, white, brown – were housed; the prostitutes, the pimps, the broke artists and the ultra-orthodox, all searching for a better life here or in the hereafter.'[3]

Janette Parris' digital drawings are defiantly described by the artist as the opposite of a memoir. Drawn from her forthcoming artist's book *This is Not a Memoir*, 2023, which she describes as a 'graphic A–Z for East and South London', Parris evokes the style of comic books and graphic novels to create a series of vibrant digital drawings. The works included in the exhibition humorously map locations in the East End which are of significance in the artist's personal life but also in a wider social history of London. Parris' chosen sites mark important locations in the artist's life journey: the Ilford Palais, the first nightclub the artist attended; the old Upton Park stadium of her beloved football team, West Ham; the Royal Mail Sorting Office in Farringdon where she worked night shifts alongside completing a fine art degree at Goldsmiths College; the Granada television rental shop; and the Boleyn Cinema in East Ham where she first saw Stanley Kubrick's *2001: A Space Odyssey*. Through wry and comic commentaries on her own life and experiences, Parris simultaneously charts the pleasures and struggles of working-class life in East London from night-shift working, which induces exhaustion and illness, to the joys of disco-dancing late into the night. Parris skilfully interweaves her personal evolution into an artist with the transformation of popular landmarks and locations in East London.

A constellation of manhole-cover-like iron casts, originally conceived as a site-specific public sculpture, William Cobbing's *Written in Water,* 2022, is embedded in the paving along the banks of the Hertford Union Canal on Fish Island. Displaying the original moulds across the upper floor of Whitechapel Gallery, each mould is embossed with a short text which conjures up East End lives, past and present, and speaks to the diversity and precarity of the local area: 'The local culture emerges from between the cracks in the pavements, as with Bashy's gleeful recollection of the notoriously dilapidated Déjà Vu pirate station in Waterden Road. These places, often in derelict warehouses and vacated factories, provided temporary homes for counterculture, most of which disappeared as the area was developed when the Olympics arrived in Stratford on the east bank of the River Lea'.[4] Like ripples on the surface of the water, these fragile histories risk disappearing forever. The unrelenting cycles of radical change and upheaval threaten to bury the stories and lives which Cobbing has retrieved and amplified:

BARGEMEN GAZED OUT AT MR GANDHI FROM THEIR NIGHTWORK AS HE WALKED ALONG THE LEA FROM KINGSLEY HALL; THE NAVIES DREDGING MUD WOULD SHOUT THEIR GREETING.[5]

BRIDGET AND I CAME DOWN TO THE EAST END FOR A DRINK. WE SAW A GUY FITTING OUT HIS BOAT BY A DERELICT WAREHOUSE, WITH GREAT OPEN SPACES FOR STUDIOS.[6]

SHE USED TO ROW TEN OF THEM IN A LONG BOAT ACROSS THE CANAL TO THE PUB BY CLARINCO'S ALL OF THEM ON THE BEER. THEN ROW BACK, CHARGE 'EM A PENNY A TIME.[7]

WHEN LOCKDOWN BEGAN A DOCTOR ASKED HACKNEY WICK MUTUAL AID FOR HELP TO SEW MEDICAL SCRUBS, SO WE DESIGNED A PATTERN AND RALLIED VOLUNTEERS TO MAKE THEM.[8]

The streets of East London are the setting for Mitra Tabrizian's *Film Stills*, 2017–2018, a series of C-type photographic prints. While film stills are customarily photographs of the main character or characters, taken on a film set to introduce and publicise a film, Tabrizian's film stills deviate from that approach. Inspired by her feature film *Gholam* (2018), which tells the story of an enigmatic Iranian taxi driver in London, Tabrizian focuses on actors rejected from the cast, extras, and empty landscapes. Playing on the formal and structural qualities of film- and image-making, Tabrizian invites us to consider the relationship between what is 'within the frame' – central, included and dominating our attention – and what lies 'out-of-the-frame' – excluded, superfluous and out of view. As with her film *Gholam*, Tabrizian's collection of images leave the narrative open to interpretation, portraying 'the "unseen" city of migrants, living on the edge – and the sense of being on the "other-side"'.[9] There are those who are central to the unfolding narrative and those who circulate at its edges. In spite of the gap between them, they depend on and shape each others lives.

John Smith's seminal film *The Girl Chewing Gum*, 1976, wittily undermines mainstream cinema by drawing attention to its artifice rather than attempting to disguise it. Shot continuously on 16-mm black-and-white film at an intersection near a cinema in Hackney, a voice-over of the artist appears to direct the action in a busy London street. The artist's 'direction' of the movements of passers-by becomes steadily more absurd when Smith starts to direct pigeons and the hour hand of a clock. Decades after the film was made, it has acquired new layers of meaning. Smith's parody of the idea of the filmmaker as an all-powerful figure, who determines the action in which participants have no agency, resonates with contemporary concerns about the manipulation of power and the media to proliferate fake news. As the artist notes, the film has also become 'an almost exotic record of a distant time, where passers-by look like actors in period costumes, a difference made even more apparent by the ongoing gentrification of the film's East London location. To many young people the film looks like a relic from the early days of cinema, confirmed by school student blogs I have encountered which state that the black-and-white film, composed of only two shots, was made before colour film was invented, and before filmmakers learnt how to edit."[10]

Reflecting poetically on *Fatima's Letter*, 1992, the artist Alia Syed writes: 'London is never London but contains traces of other cities, the poignancy of the landscape lies in its ability to conjure, the sound of a horn, Karachi – one city falls into another.' Shot almost entirely at Whitechapel underground station, Syed's film revolves around a woman who remembers her past from faces she sees while travelling on the London Underground. The story, which takes the form of a letter to her friend Fatima, is spoken in Urdu with subtitles in English, although the subtitles do not always appear in conjunction with what is spoken and it is impossible to grasp the narrative which unfolds in fragments. Shadows and reflections flit continuously across the screen and the only constant seems to be Whitechapel train station, through which countless bodies and sounds flow unceasingly. London collapses into Karachi and the past falls into the present. As viewers of Syed's film, we cannot help but also feel disorientated and displaced, unsure of where we are and what we can hold onto.

Working with paint rather than film, Jerome's *Action Black*, 2018–Present, engages with how living moments can be captured and expressed through the medium of paint. After applying glossy black paint to vinyl flooring and allowing it to dry, the artist 'exposes' the vinyl flooring to various events where participants are invited to write what they are feeling on the flooring, and to walk on and stress the surface of the floorboards. Over the course of successive events – a fashion show, a Black Lives Matter protest, dinners and performances – the flooring acquires traces of lived experience that activate the work. The paint is later stripped from the floorboards and used as a medium within the artist's *Action Black* paintings. Jerome describes the different stages through which the work evolves as 'pre-activation, activation, post-activation and re-activation.' Jerome moves intentionally away from the idea of action painting as a singular act or gesture of applying paint to canvas, limited to the artist himself. Rather, these works are contingent on the actions and words of others, setting the works in motion. For Jerome *Action Black* adds 'another angle to the conversation that Pierre Soulages' *Outrenoir* (Beyond Black) paintings beautifully address [...] but instead utilises the lived experience of the black paint, capturing something living, something important and something now all at the same time.'[11]

Matthew Krishanu's enigmatic figurative paintings *Bows and Arrows*, 2018, *Boy on a Climbing Frame*, 2022, and *Four Children (Verandah)*, 2022, do not depict specific individuals or events but rather evoke a mood or atmosphere which is often ambiguous and troubling: two boys armed with sling bows, apparently about to take aim and fire; the boy frozen at the top of a climbing frame who may be fixed in fear, or about to jump; and the children waiting expectantly for something to happen, or perhaps belligerently confronting us, the viewers? Like a writer who synthesises the manners and gestures of different people to fashion fictional characters, Krishanu distils memories of people, places and events in his personal history to create paintings which collapse time and geography. By contrast, Krishanu's series of paintings *In Sickness and In Health*, 2007–2022, emerge from a specific period of time and hugely significant relationship in the artist's life. Made by Krishanu over the course of more than a decade of a life spent together with the writer Uschi Gatward before her untimely death from cancer in late 2021, the paintings chart Gatward's life journey through marriage, childbirth, motherhood and dying. Small in scale, these intimate artworks bring together interwoven personal histories with the entangled histories of painting from Gwen John and Edward Hopper to Frida Kahlo and Indian miniature painting.

Filmed from the artist's window during the first COVID-19 lockdown, John Smith's incisive and playful *Citadel*, 2020, combines short fragments from the speeches British Prime Minister Boris Johnson made during the coronavirus pandemic with views of the London skyline. *Citadel* is a damning indictment of the privileging of business interests over public health. While Smith's camera remains fixed in place, the weather and light constantly change as we move from day to night, from winter to summer. As the pandemic unfolds and the death toll rises, the film shifts its focus from the city's gleaming skyscrapers to the inhabitants of the dense urban housing that lies in their shadow. Smith's camera picks out mundane, night-time scenes of life under lockdown. Vermeer-like vignettes spotlight a woman exercising in her living room, a man working on his laptop, a couple washing up and clearing the kitchen after a meal. In the eerie, evening cityscape of lockdown, electric lighting seems to take on a life of its own, first of all, mirroring Boris Johnson's speech patterns in a newly-completed office block in Bishopsgate and then flashing on and off to spell out SOS in Morse code in adjacent domestic housing.

Curtains of powder-coated chain-link fencing are suspended from the ceiling of the upper gallery of the Whitechapel Gallery to create a coloured metal structure which is, by turns, playful and menacing. Rana Begum's *No. 1272 Chainlink*, 2023, continues the artist's interest in blurring the boundaries between painting, sculpture, design and architecture. Responding to the ubiquity of fencing material in the landscape, which is used to enclose everything from domestic suburban properties to high-security military compounds, Begum has adopted and transformed chain-link fencing into material for a series of installations and sculptures. The artist skilfully manipulates its form and colour to neutralise its violent association with closed borders and insurmountable barriers. Begum renders it as a constantly shifting structure, altering with the variations in natural light and the movement of the viewer: 'I want the works to be constantly something that spark curiosity, throwing up questions. I love trying to find that balance between where an artwork is neither one thing nor another, and celebrating the fact that it can be both. A work can be made from a heavy and weighty material, for example, but in the way that it looks it can imply that it is light and full of air. I enjoy that constant battle, that grinding between the two.'[12]

Susan Hiller's two related works *The J. Street Project (Index)*, 2002–2005, and *The J. Street Project (Film)*, 2002–2005, came out of a DAAD residency in Berlin in 2002–2003. Walking around the city, the artist came across a street sign bearing the name *Judenstrasse* (Jews' Street). Hiller was shocked and confused to find a street name intended as a respectful commemoration which in fact was a commemoration of a complex history of racism, segregation and violence. Over the next three years, the artist mapped every German street, lane, alley and avenue with the prefix 'Juden' in its name. *The J. Street Project (Index)*, 2002–2005, is an installation made up of 303 colour photographs hung in a massive grid and accompanied by a large-scale map of Germany with each location listed and pinpointed. *The J. Street Project (Film)*, 2002–2005, presents a sequence of static camera shots of these inner-city shopping streets, dreamy lanes, anonymous suburbs, and secluded country roads, as the soundtrack records traffic noise, church bells and other incidental sounds. 'All my work deals with ghosts,' Hiller has said and these works powerfully articulate how Germany's past continues to haunt the present. The quotidian and mundane nature of these streets and alleys merely heightens the dissonance between the banality of the present and the violent and traumatic past to which they testify: 'A photographic image can only, ever, represent things as they are in the present moment when the image is "taken". But the present is a summation of everything that precedes it and each photograph will be seen in the context of everything that happens afterwards. In that way, *The J. Street Project* has allowed me to reflect not only on one unique, incurable, traumatic absence, but also on more recent attempts to destroy minority cultures and erase their presence.'[13]

Like Hiller's *The J. Street Project*, Sarah Dobai's single-screen film *The Donkey Field*, 2021, similarly reflects on how historical events in the past continue to resonate and reverberate in the present. The film weaves a link between a racist attack on a young boy on a piece of common land, known locally as 'the donkey field', and the story of the persecution of Marie and the donkey Balthazar in Robert Bresson's film *Au Hasard Balthazar* (1966). Dobai's film features a text based on sections of a memoir of Budapest in the last year of World War II, and scenes which re-enact and re-frame Bresson's allegorical story about the scapegoating of innocent subjects: 'The making of the film', writes Dobai, 'was prompted by recognising the historical echo of the refugee crisis in Europe, to the plight of Jews in World War II. Particularly relevant to this was the report of an episode in 2015 at Keleti Station, in Budapest, where refugees from Syria and Afghanistan were kettled and then herded onto a train, apparently bound for Munich, and then, to their terror, forced off into a camp in the middle of the Hungarian Plains.'[14]

Made over twenty years ago, Mark Wallinger's *Threshold to the Kingdom*, 2000, takes on renewed significance in relation to increasingly intolerant and inhumane measures in recent years to stem the flow of migrants and refugees crossing England's borders. Shot in a single take from a fixed position at London's eastern City Airport, *Threshold to the Kingdom* is a single channel colour video projection which tracks arrivals to the airport in slow-motion footage, accompanied by a soundtrack of *Miserere*, a seventeenth-century setting of the fifty-first psalm in the Bible by the Italian composer Gregorio Allegri (c.1582–1652). Wallinger sets up a playful equivalence between crossing the highly-controlled and monitored state threshold into the United Kingdom and crossing a religious threshold into the Kingdom of Heaven: 'In negotiating the more or less authoritarian or coercive apparatus of the state which define and control one's progress from 'air-side' to land-side', one is perhaps reminded of a kind of secular equivalent of the progression from confession to absolution. Eventually, all that separates us from the no-man's land and the official terra firma of the state are a pair of automatic doors.'[15]

Positioned adjacent to the exit from the upper galleries at Whitechapel Gallery, Wallinger's film is a powerful reminder of the inequities between those who have free, unproblematic passage to travel and cross borders and those whose routes are precarious and life-threatening. London is never London, as Alia Syed writes, not only because it contains the traces of other cities but also because its inhabitants experience vastly different versions of the city which frequently sit cheek by jowl. The works assembled in this exhibition create an archaeology of the present which, to paraphrase Susan Hiller, are a summation of everything that precedes them and will be seen in the context of everything that happens afterwards.

1
Susan Hiller, Unpublished artist's note

2
Osman Yousefzada quoted by Claudia Croft in 'Osman Yousefzada Launches a New Exhibition on the Experience of Migration', *Vogue*, 7 June 2018 (https://www.vogue.co.uk/article/osman-yousefzada-ikon-gallery-being-somewhere-else)

3
Osman Yousefzada, *The Go-Between: A Portrait of Growing Up Between Different Worlds* (London: Canongate Books, 2022)

4
William Cobbing, Artist Statement, 2023

5
Muriel Lester, 'Entertaining Gandhi', Ivor Nicholson and Watson Ltd (1932)

6
Bridget Riley and Peter Sedgley interview about their artist studio move to Martello Street and Stepney Green. Filmed by Space Studios (1970)

7
Ronnie. Transcript of recording 'Mapping the Change: Old Ford Voices and Island Memories Oral History', Tower Hamlets Local History Library and Archive (2011)

8
Annabel Maguire, Hackney Wick Mutual Aid Scrub Hub (2020)

9
Mitra Tabrizian, Artist Statement, 2018

10
John Smith, Artist Statement: 'On The Girl Chewing Gum and the passing of time', 2022

11
Jerome, Artist Statement, May 2023

12
Rana Begum in conversation with Lisa Le Feuvre in *Rana Begum: Space Light Colour* (London: Lund Humphires, 2021)

13
Susan Hiller, Artist Statement, 2005

14
Sarah Dobai from a talk at BALTIC, Gateshead, January 2022

15
Mark Wallinger, Artist Statement, 2000

Rana Begum

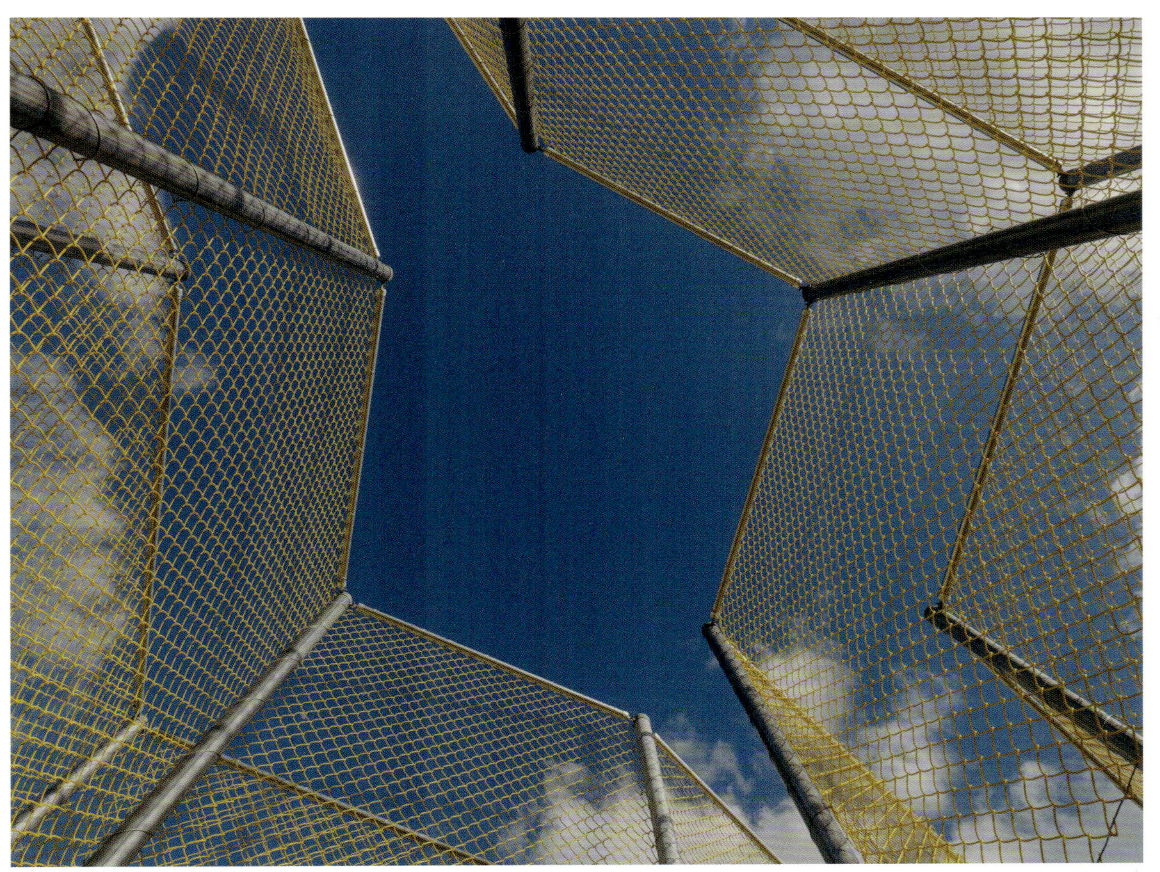

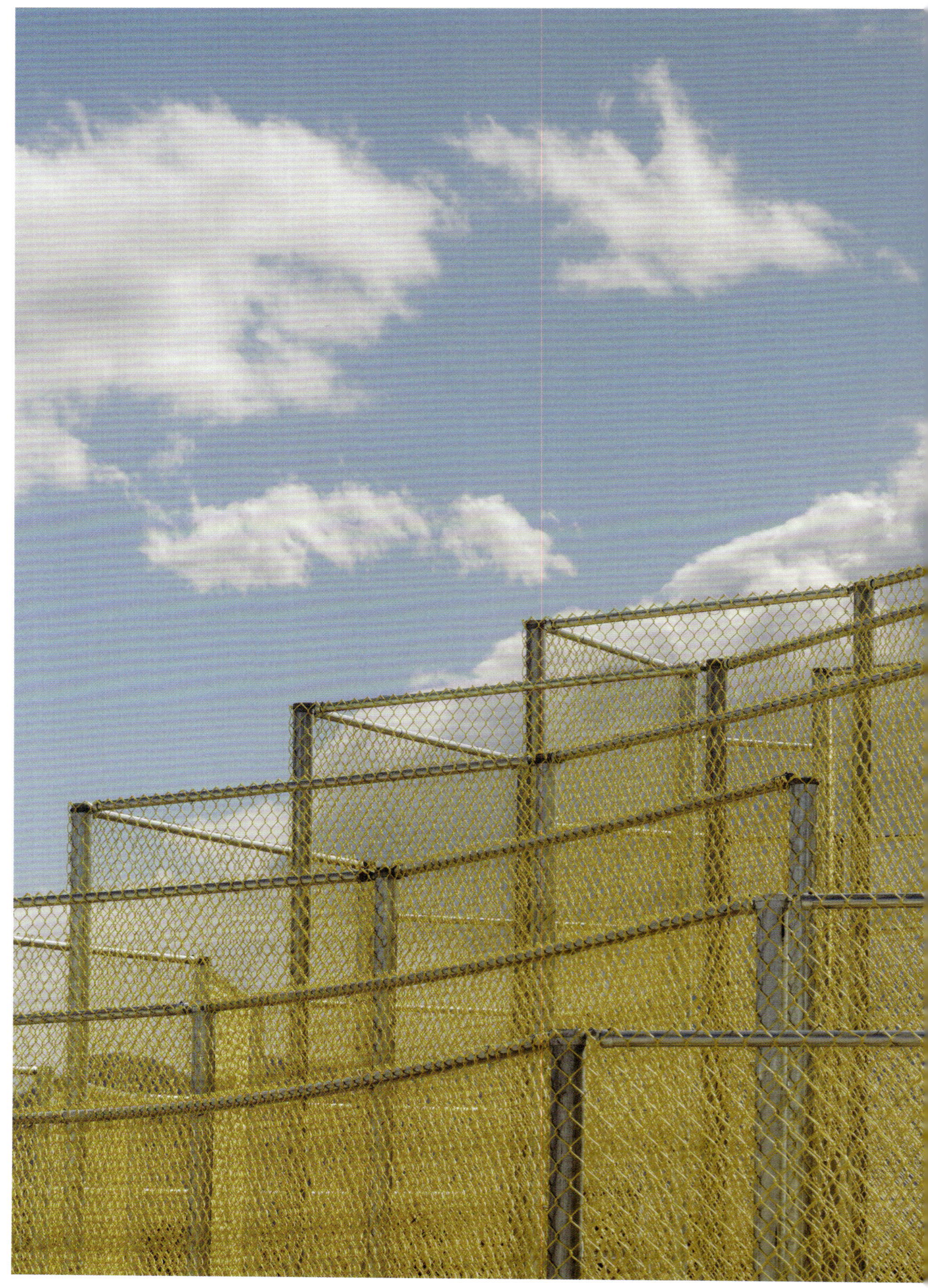

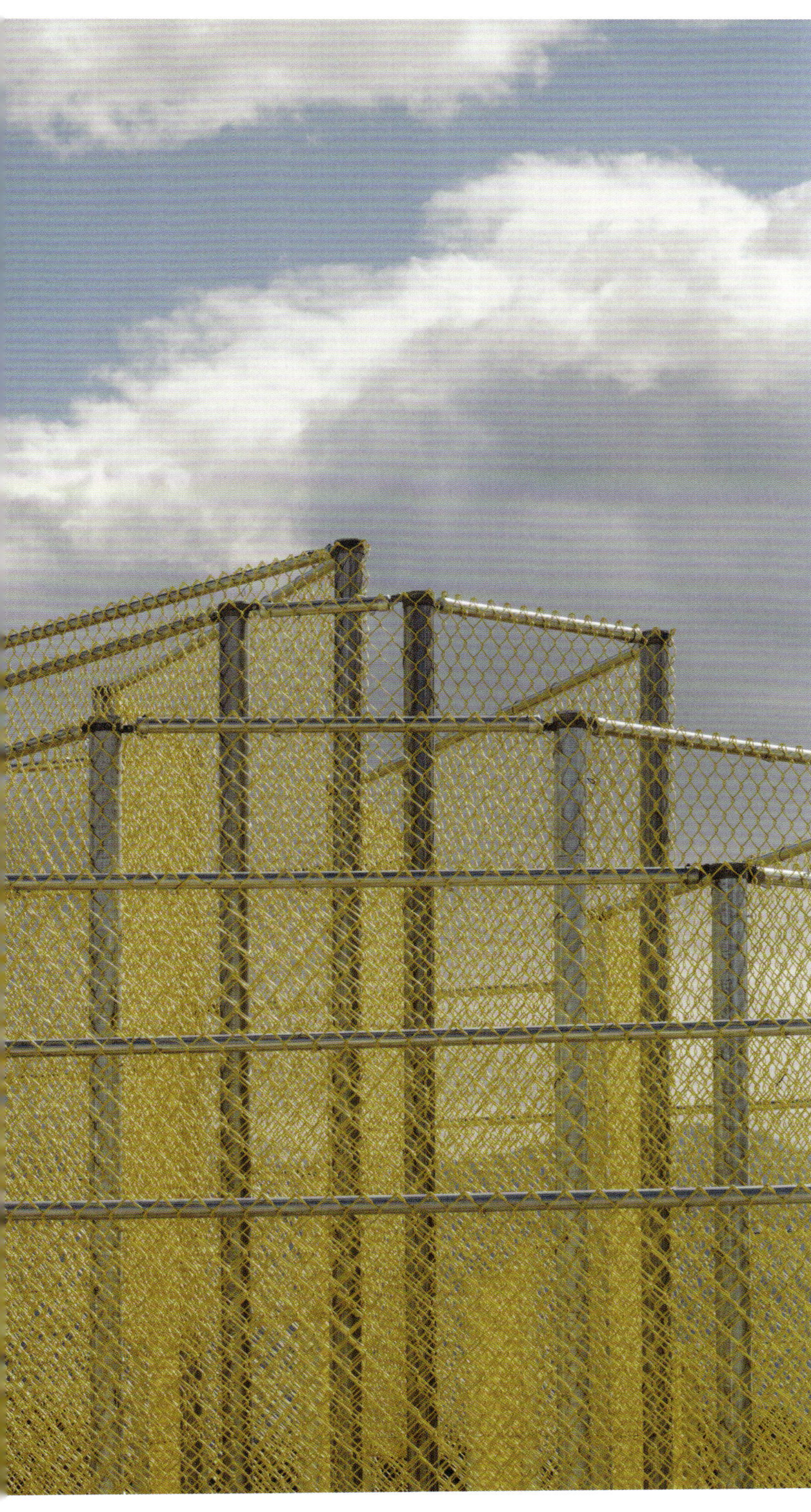

Pages 17–19
Rana Begum
No. 1225 Chainlink, Desert X
2022

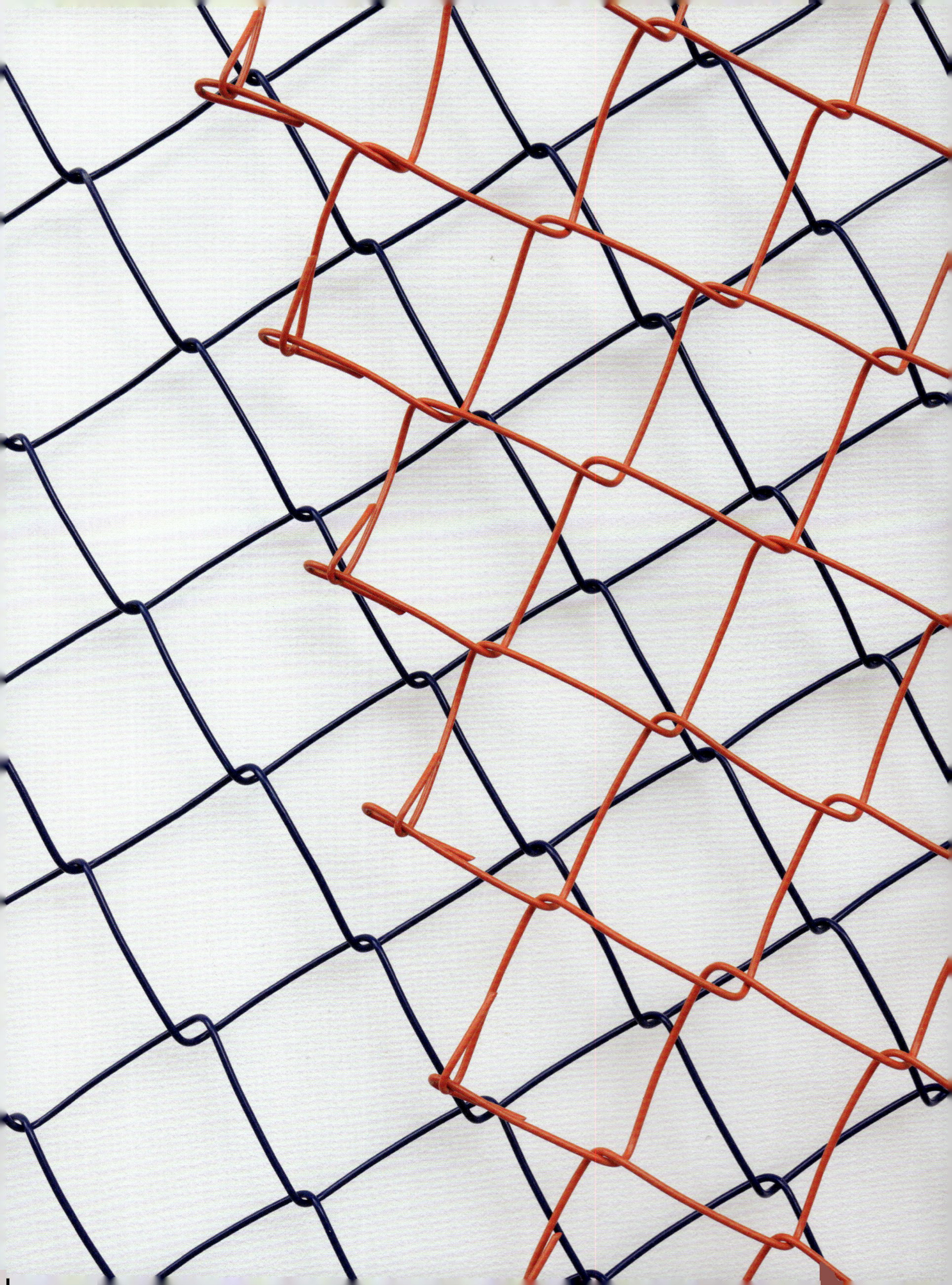

Rana Begum
No. 1242 Chainlink   2023

I want the works to be constantly something that spark curiosity, throwing up questions. I love trying to find that balance between where an artwork is neither one thing nor another, and celebrating the fact that it can be both. A work can be made from a heavy and weighty material, for example, but in the way that it looks it can imply that it is light and full of air. I enjoy that constant battle, that grinding between the two.

Excerpt from 'A Conversation with Lisa Le Feuvre; Waves of Light', *Rana Begum: Space Light Colour*, Lund Humphries, London, 2021

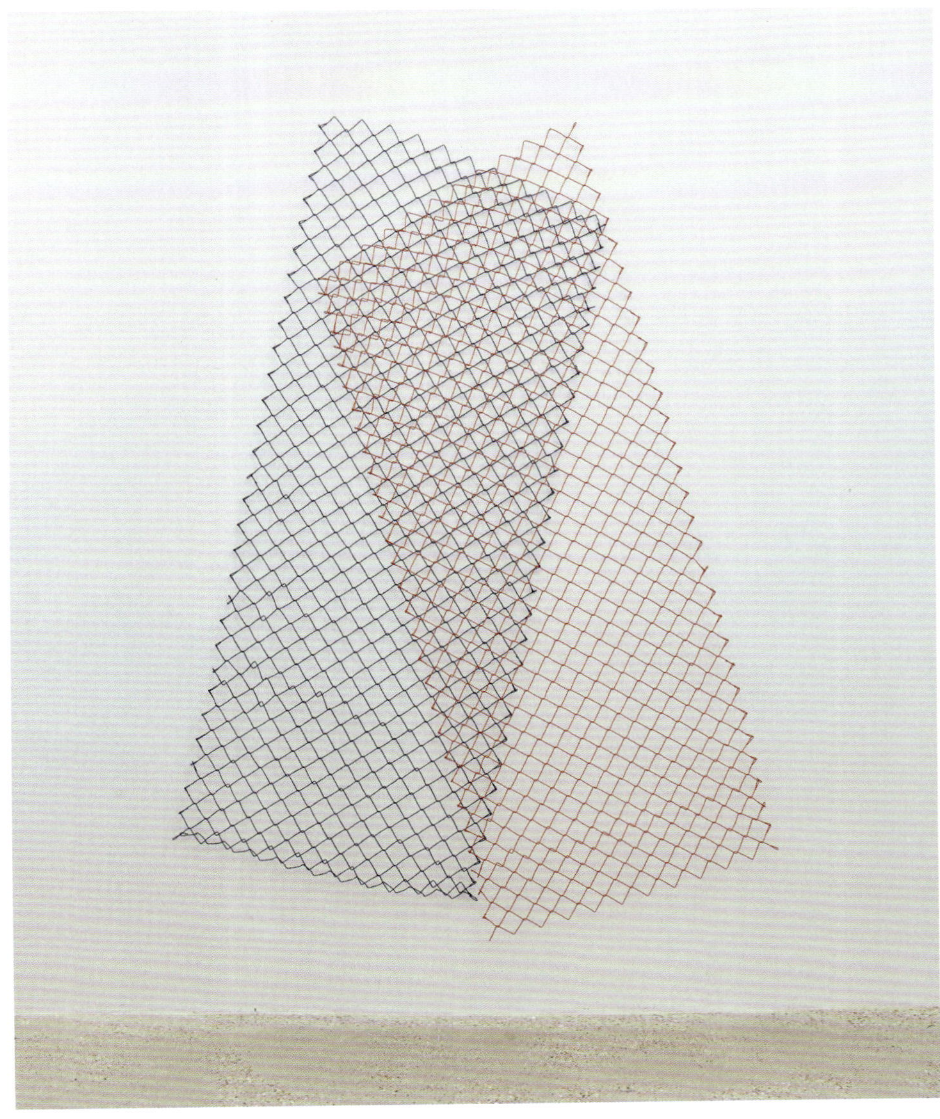

William Cobbing

William Cobbing

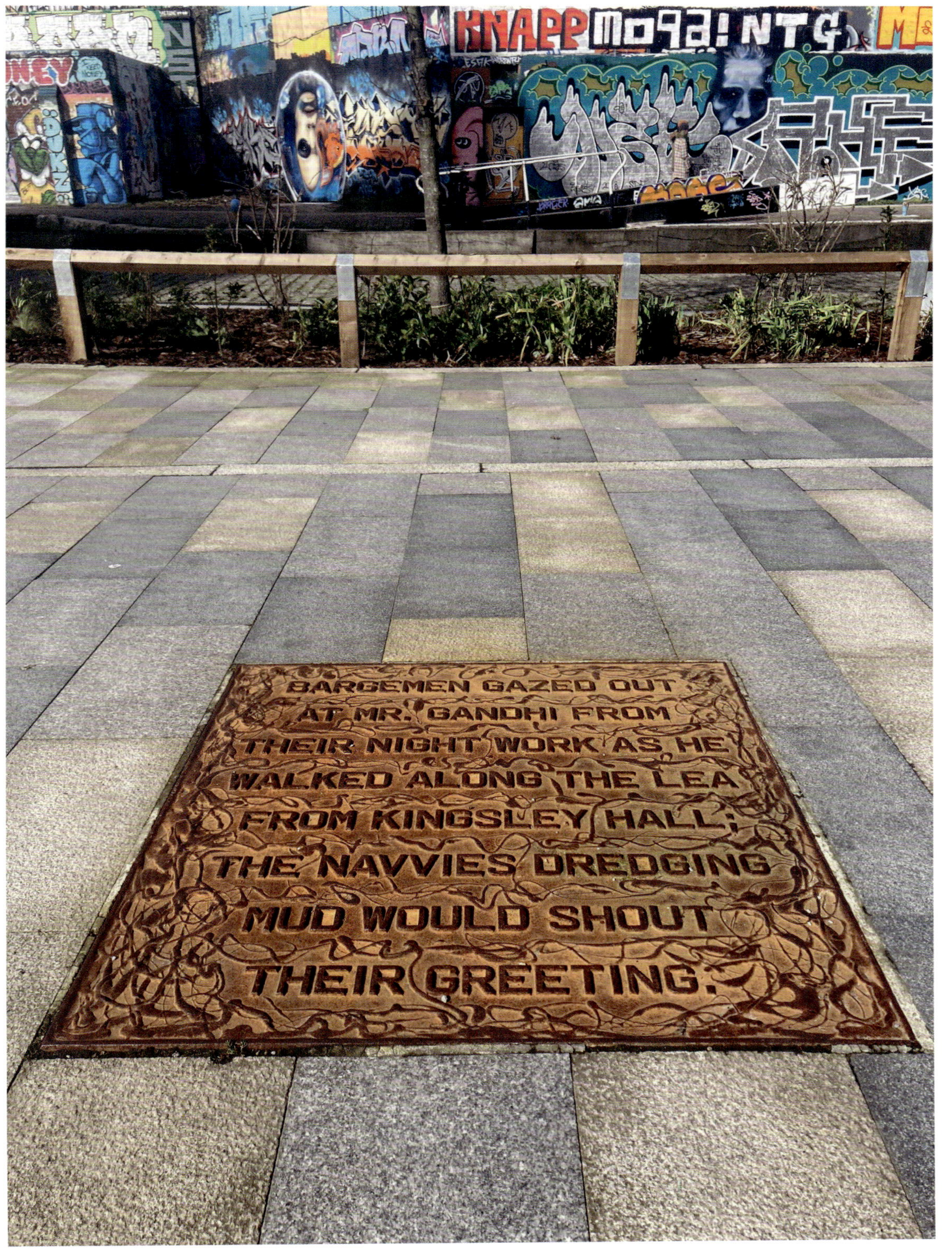

BARGEMEN GAZED OUT
AT MR. GANDHI FROM
THEIR NIGHT WORK AS HE
WALKED ALONG THE LEA
FROM KINGSLEY HALL;
THE NAVVIES DREDGING
MUD WOULD SHOUT
THEIR GREETING.

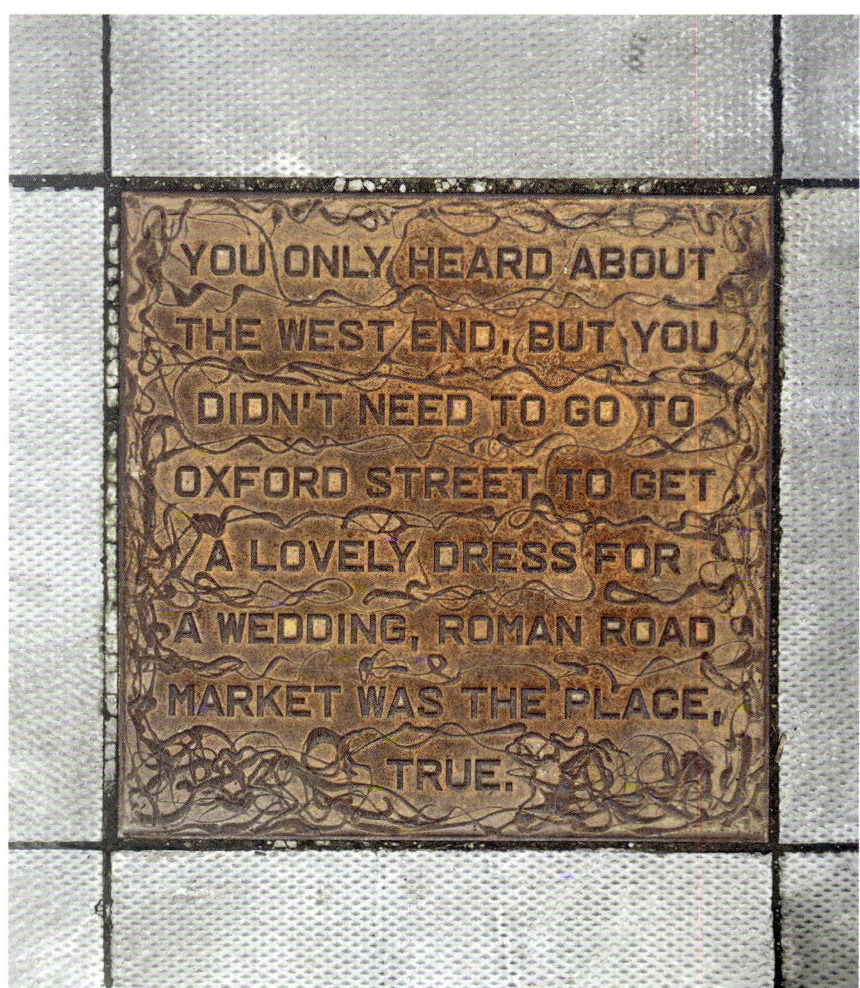

Pages 23–27   **William Cobbing**   *Written in Water*   2022

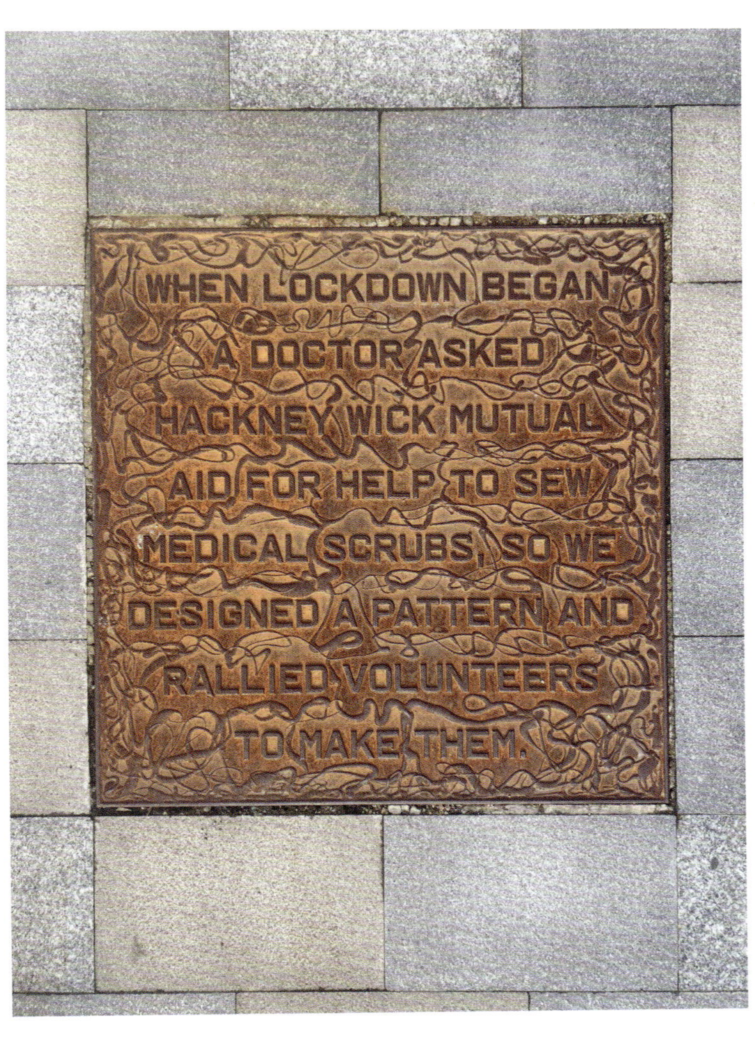

WHEN LOCKDOWN BEGAN
A DOCTOR ASKED
HACKNEY WICK MUTUAL
AID FOR HELP TO SEW
MEDICAL SCRUBS, SO WE
DESIGNED A PATTERN AND
RALLIED VOLUNTEERS
TO MAKE THEM.

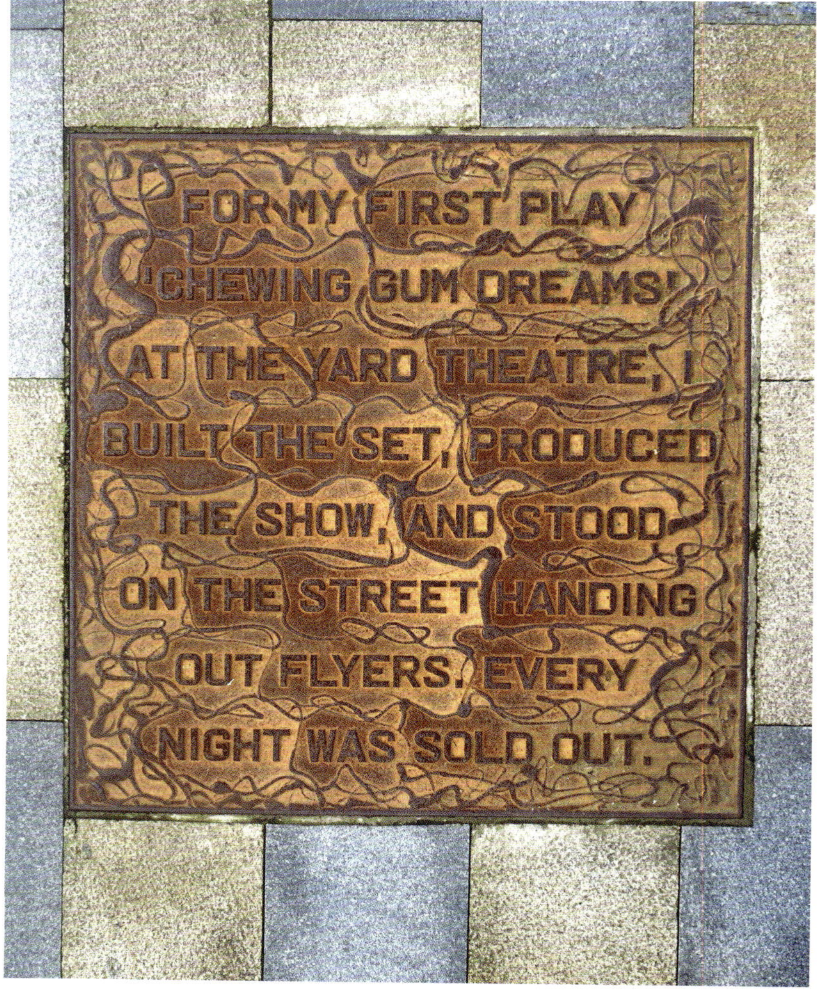
FOR MY FIRST PLAY
'CHEWING GUM DREAMS'
AT THE YARD THEATRE, I
BUILT THE SET, PRODUCED
THE SHOW, AND STOOD
ON THE STREET HANDING
OUT FLYERS. EVERY
NIGHT WAS SOLD OUT.

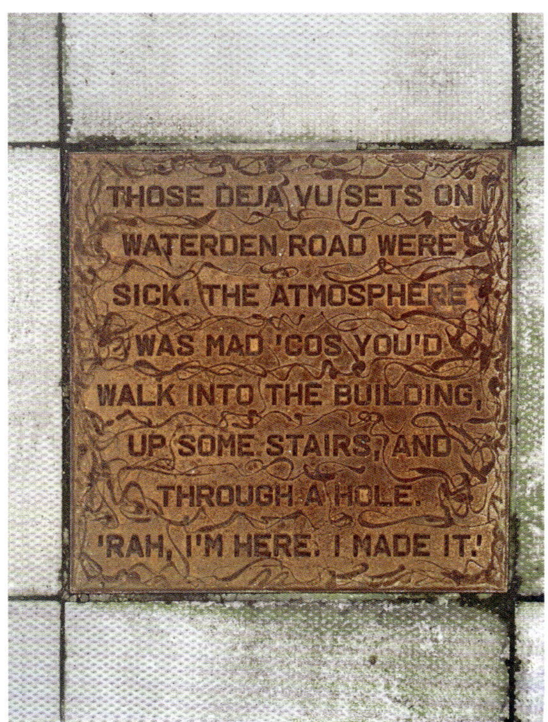

Written in Water is a new public sculpture commission consisting of ten square manhole cover-style iron casts embedded in the paving along the banks of the Hertford Union Canal on Fish Island. Each iron cast is embossed with a short text, evoking the rich diversity and precarity of the local area, both past and present.

These include a text message sent by Bobby Kasanga, the manager of local Hackney Wick FC, Michaela Coel recalling the first night of her play *Chewing Gum Dreams* at The Yard Theatre, and Bridget Riley's account of finding derelict warehouses in the east end to convert into affordable artists' studios. More historical accounts are provided by transcriptions recorded in the Tower Hamlets Library and Archive: a boy fleeing Doodlebug bombs during the Blitz by diving into the canal; a woman earning a penny by rowing locals over the River Lea to the pub by the Clarnico factory.

The title *Written in Water* is taken from the inscription on John Keats' gravestone in Rome, referencing the fleeting nature of these fragile histories in an area that has been a magnet for migration, undergoing continual cycles of radical change and upheaval. Reflecting this, the iron casts have a ripple effect, meandering across the surface of the work, in between the angular text blocks.

The local culture emerges from between the cracks in the pavements, as with Bashy's gleeful recollection of the notoriously dilapidated Deja Vu FM pirate radio station in Waterden Road. These places, often in derelict warehouses and vacated factories, provided temporary homes for counterculture, much of which disappeared as the area was developed when the Olympics arrived in Stratford on the east bank of the River Lea.

My connection to the area comes from my mother's grandparents, who emigrated from County Mayo in Ireland to Bethnal Green in the 1930s. I now have a studio in the Space Bridget Riley Studios on Fish Island, which is referenced in a text on one of the iron works. The studio lease expires next year and there is the possibility that the studios will also disappear. The circuit of displacement and precarious renewal continues.

William Cobbing, May 2023

Sarah Dobai

Sarah Dobai

The making of *The Donkey Field* was prompted by recognising the historical echo of the refugee crisis in Europe, to the plight of Jews in World War II. Particularly relevant to this was the report of an episode in 2015 at Keleti Station, Budapest. Refugees from Syria and Afghanistan were kettled and then herded onto a train, apparently bound for Munich, and then, to their terror, forced off into a camp in the middle of the Hungarian Plains.

The text in the film is based on a family memoir of Budapest in 1944. The opening section tells of a racist attack on a piece of common land. The common land was known as the donkey field.

The boy, J, is shocked to discover his Jewish identity, which had been hidden from him by his parents – who hoped that this could protect him from the impact of the brutal antisemitic laws. Though the text is based closely on the factual account, all dates and most names of people, groups and places have been removed or substituted to allow the story to resonate in other historical contexts.

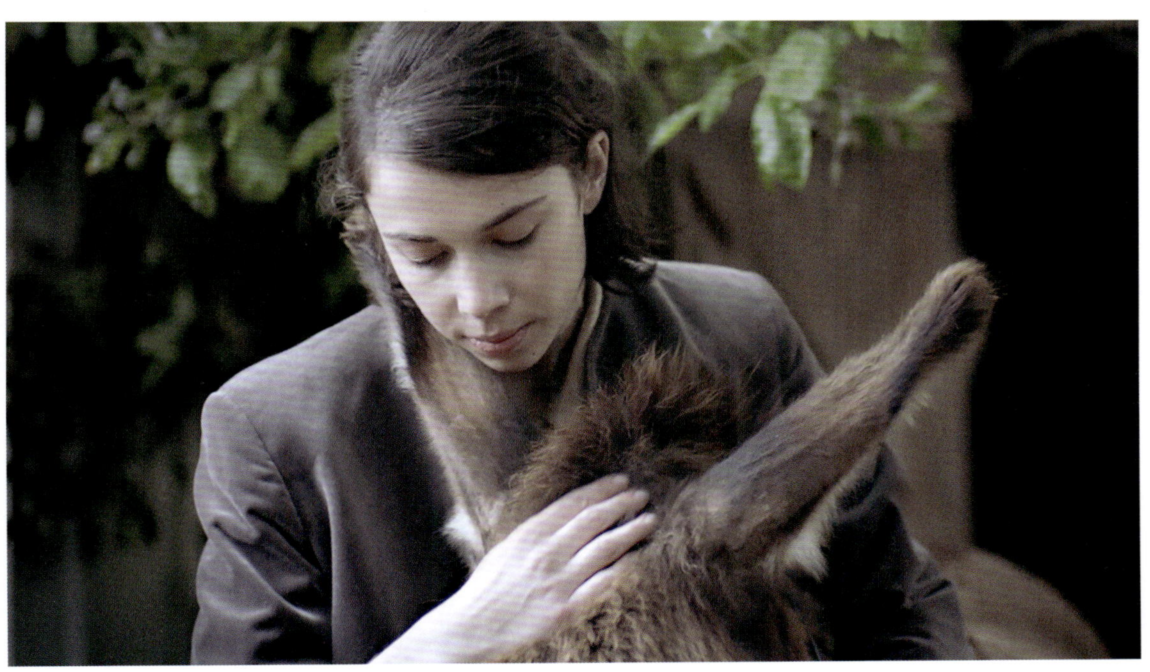

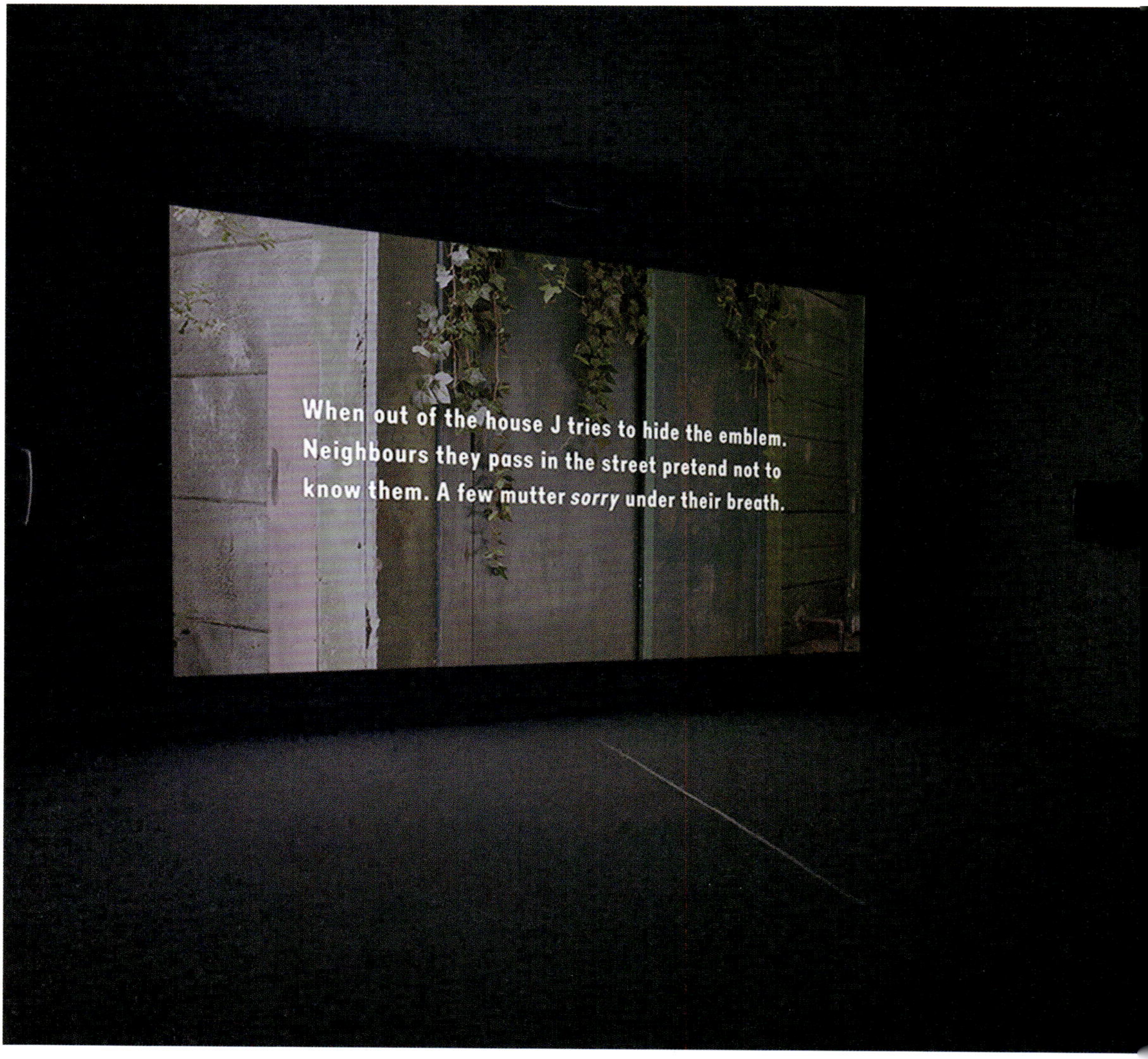

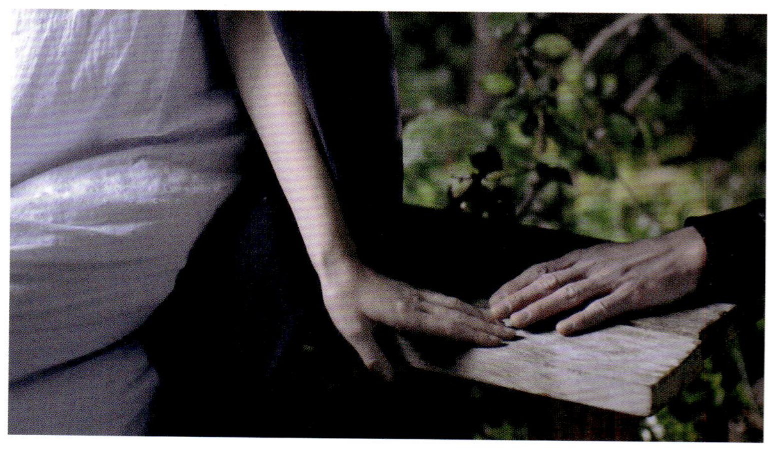

Pages 29–31
Sarah Dobai
The Donkey Field   2021

The images in the film re-enact and re-frame passages from Robert Bresson's iconic film *Au Hasard Balthazar* (1966), which centres on the story of a young girl and her donkey Balthazar. Bresson's film follows these innocent subjects, as their situation worsens, becoming the targets of a local group of thugs. I saw his film as a kind of cinematic allegory about the victimisation of blameless subjects and my reference to this classic piece of European cinema in *The Donkey Field* reflects my sense of this history as a collective legacy.

The decision to put the text and the images together came about not only through the name of the piece of common land where the attack occurred, and some lyrical links, but in seeing parallels between the film narrative and the memoir. The family memoir describes J and his mother being driven against their will across the city into ever more perilous and bleak situations; in the same way Balthazar is bought, sold or stolen – passing from one brutal owner to another. By such means the status of the donkey and the girl merge with J and his mother, just as the bully boys and their dog becomes synonymous with the fascist authorities.

Sarah Dobai

Excerpt from artist talk, BALTIC, Gateshead, January 2022

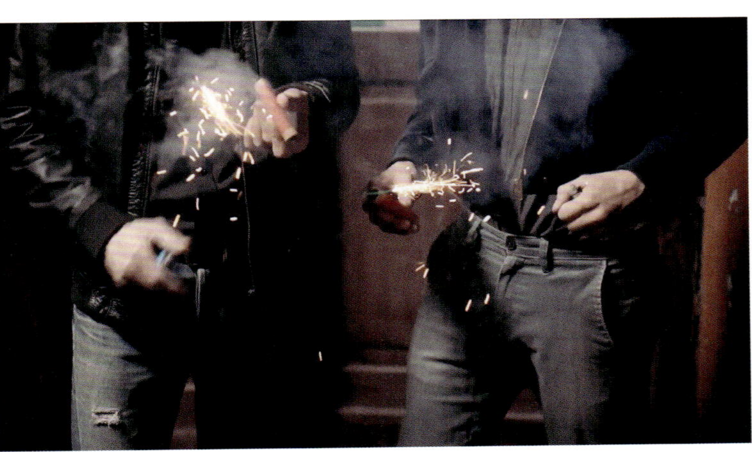

Susan Hiller

Susan Hiller

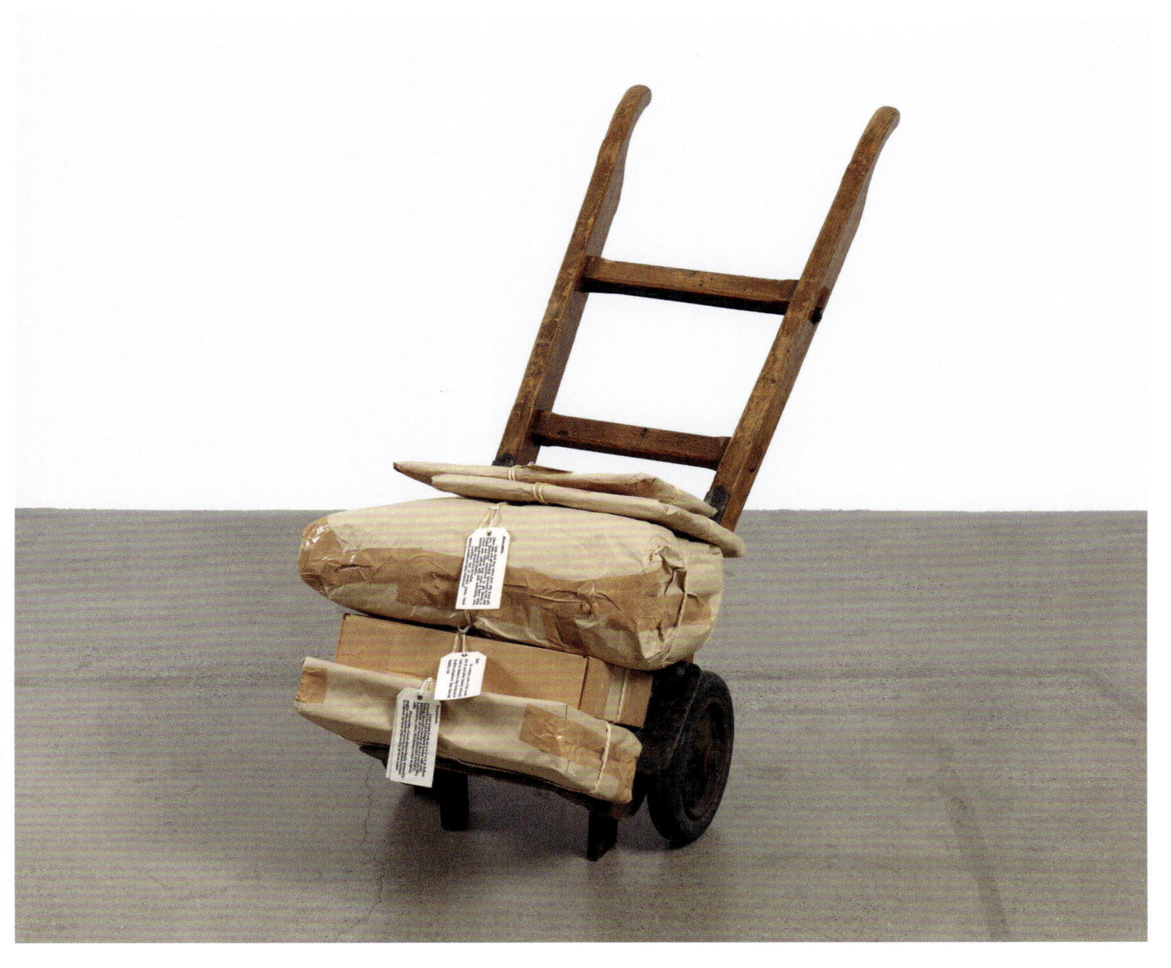

Page 33
Susan Hiller
Untitled   1999

The parcels contain items I found in the muddy
gutter of a street in London's East End, apparently
discarded during demolition of a building that
once housed a tiny shop-front synagogue. Three
of them are remnants of ritual objects: a bimah
curtain, a Torah cover, and an altar cloth. The
fourth is a large leather-bound ledger from the
synagogue's defunct burial society, into which I
inserted an old monograph about the numerous
'small synagogues' that once served London's
Jewish immigrant community. The parcels are
placed on an old-fashioned wooden peddler's
pushcart, which I had also found discarded
in the East End, because I felt all these items
were somehow in transit – from having been
in a context of meaning, where they meant
something important and specific, to some
unknown destination.

All the parcels are wrapped up and tied, with
labels that describe their contents in a museo-
logical style. A soundtrack of ritualistic singing
plays, at intervals, from a fifth parcel: fragments
of the Jewish morning prayer thanking God for
having been given a soul. By analogy, the
truthfulness of the labels of the wrapped parcels
and their significance has to be taken on faith,
because what's inside, like the soul, isn't visible.

Susan Hiller, 1999

Pages 35–37   **Susan Hiller**   *The J. Street Project (Index)*   2002–2005

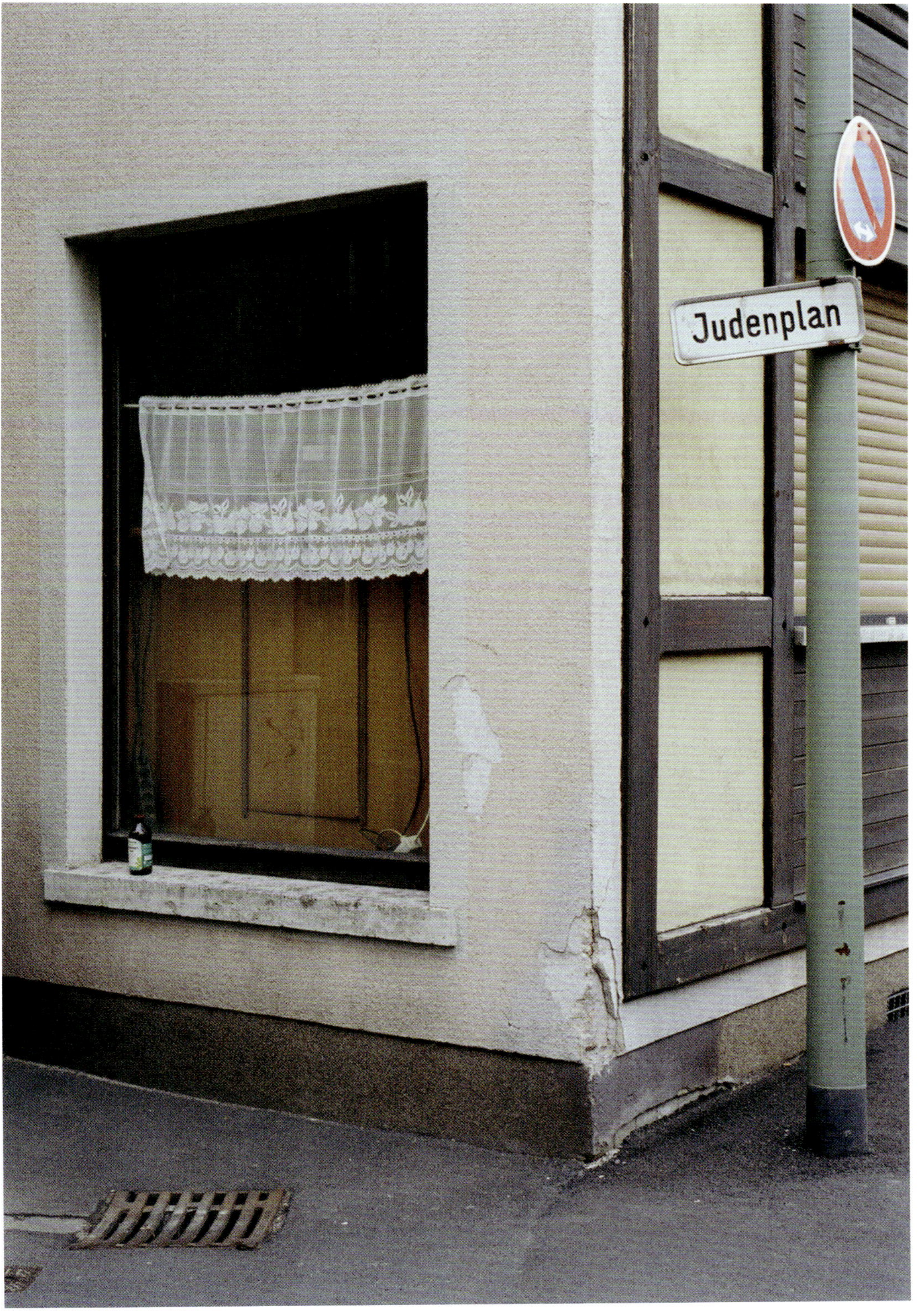
Judenplan

128

135

142

129

136

143

130

137

144

131

138

145

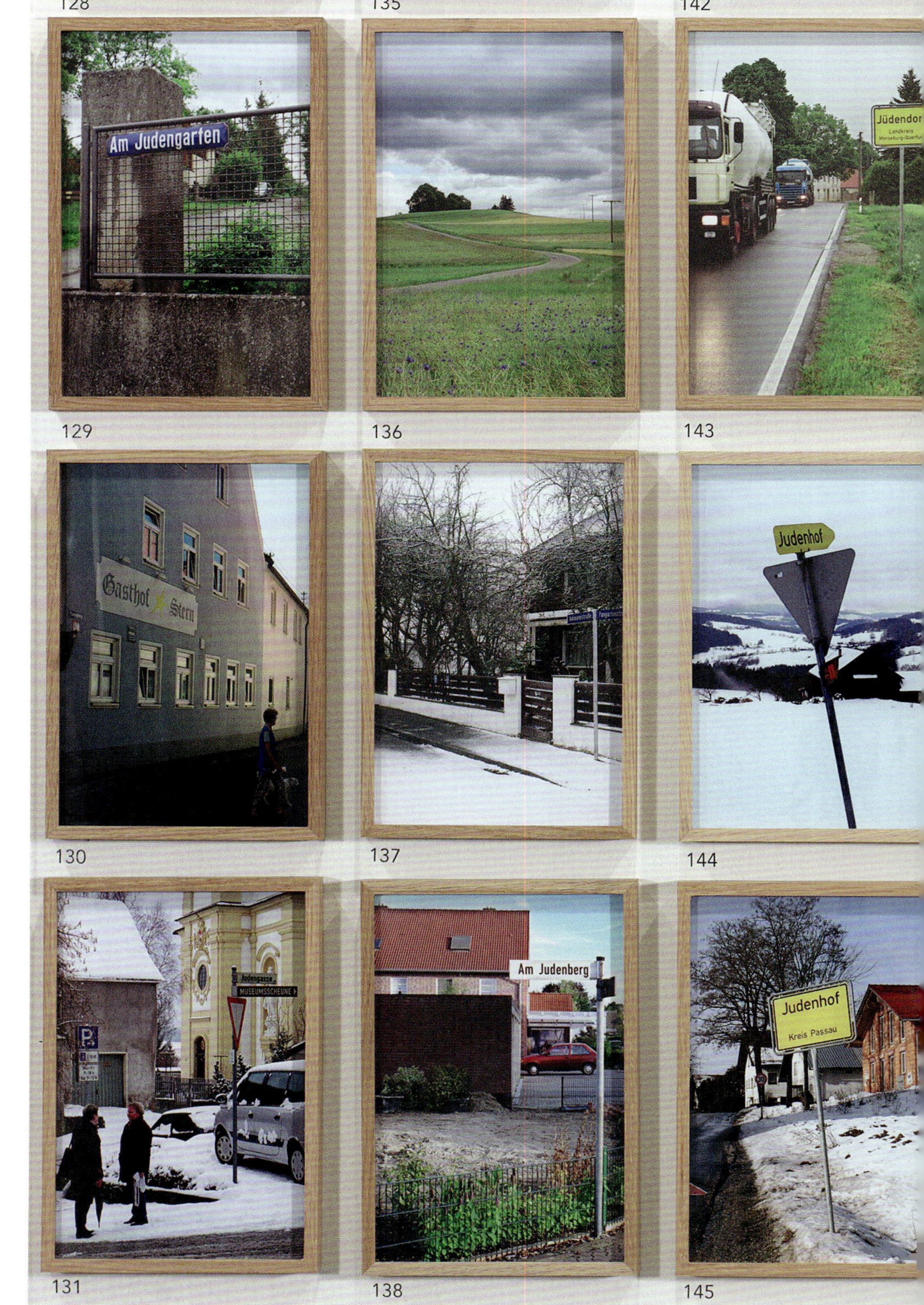

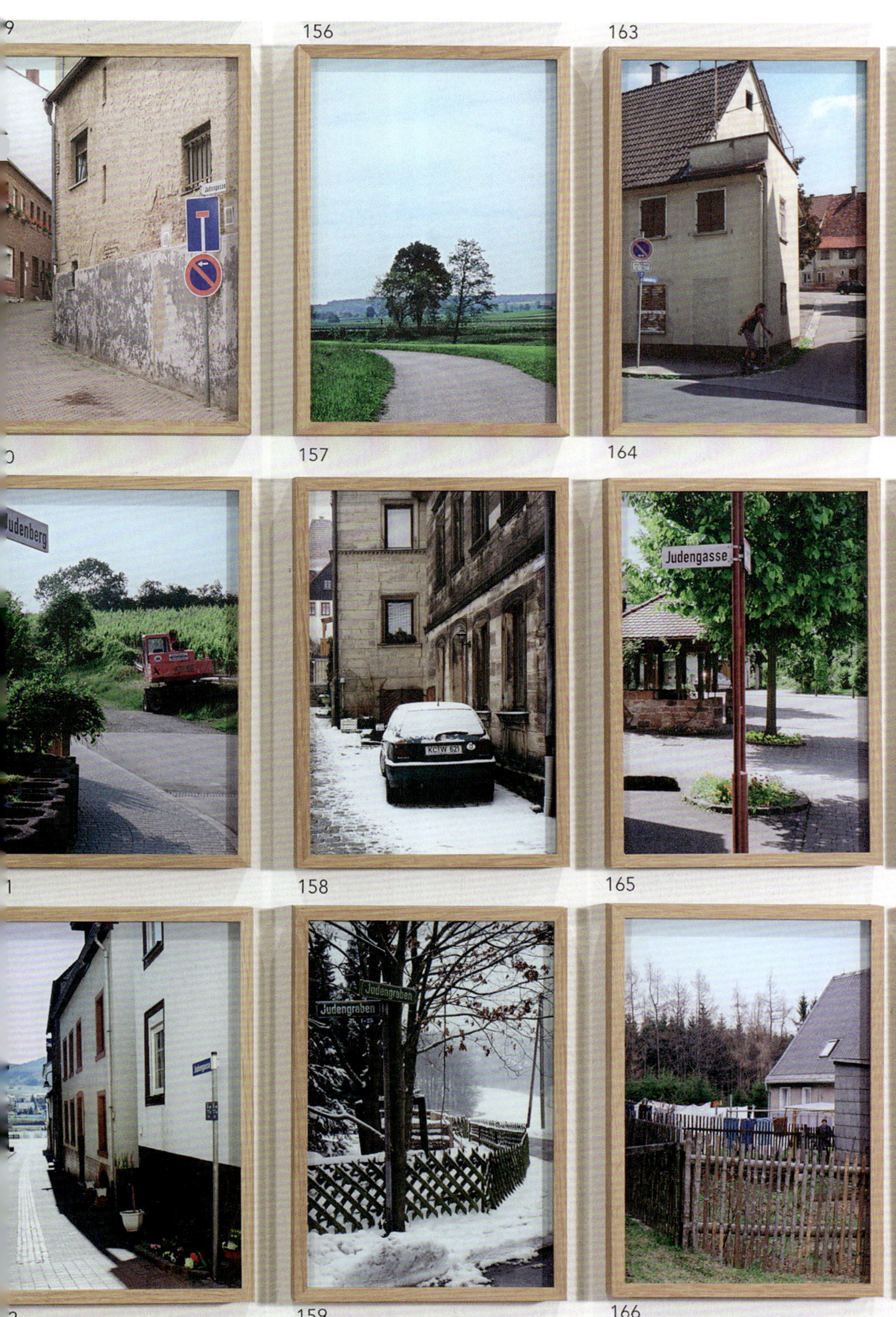

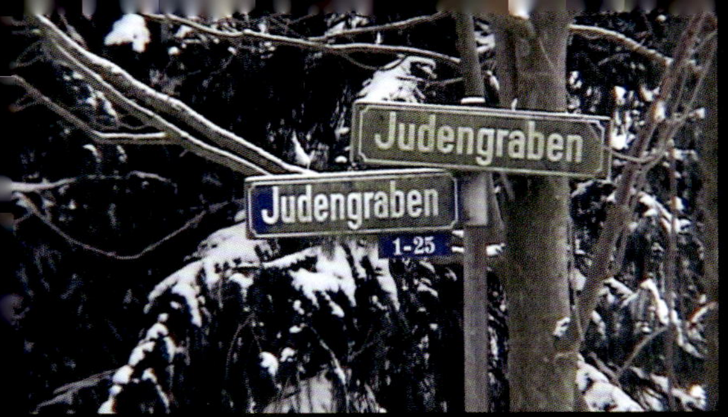

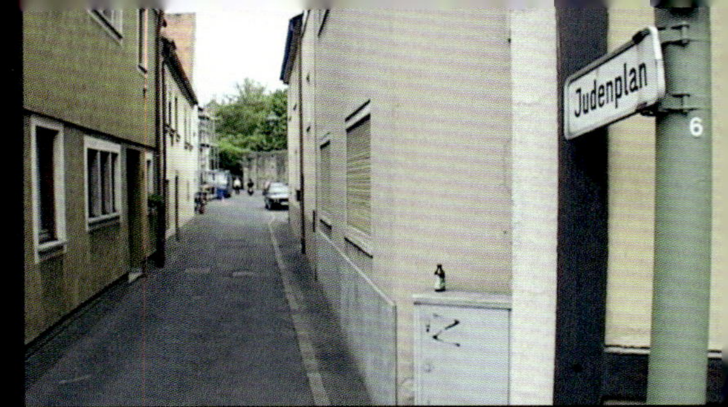

All my work deals with ghosts. *The J. Street Project* is no exception. It began as a chance encounter with a Berlin street called "Judenstraße" (Jews' Street) in 2002. When I first noticed the street sign, I was shocked, astonished but most of all, confused. I had a powerful, mixed reaction, a feeling that although the name was clearly meant as a respectful commemoration, what in fact was being commemorated was a complicated history involving racism, segregation, and violence. There seemed to be a strange ambiguity in retaining or restoring the name of a street whose former inhabitants had been exterminated within living memory.

I decided to look more carefully at these street signs, since, in my opinion, an artist's job is to look hard at things. I began travelling around Germany in search of them. In the three years it took to complete *The J. Street Project*, I travelled to tiny hamlets, famous cities and boring suburbs searching for places that are still named after their former Jewish residents. I wanted to find all of them. There was no list to consult and no guidebook. Many of the streets and roads I located on old maps had disappeared, and it surprised me to discover that more than 300 of them still exist. The Jews are gone but the street names remain as ghosts of the past, haunting

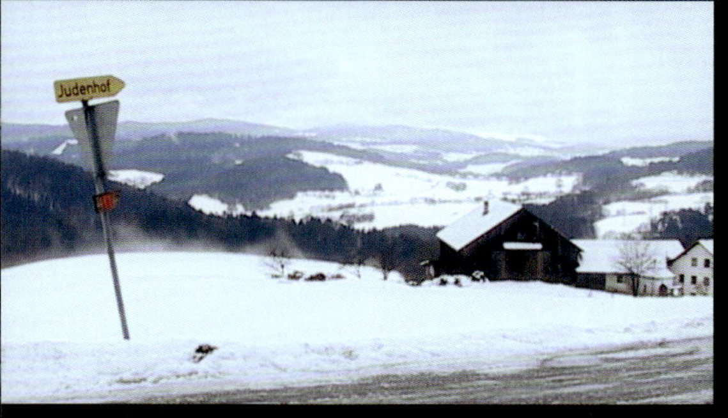

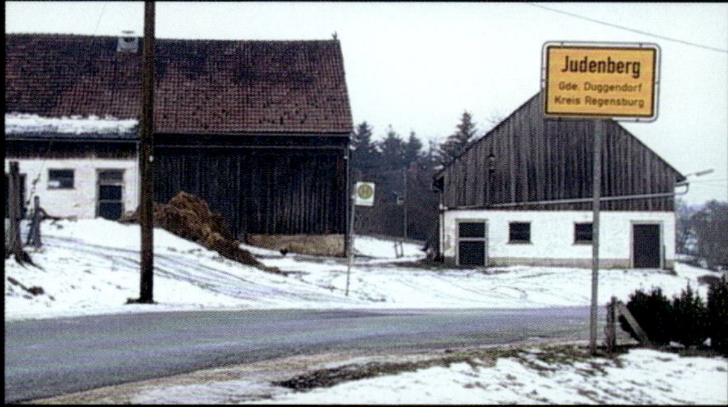

On each street, my camera recorded incidental and transient details: weather, shoppers, landscape, buildings, cars, cows, children. It's their everyday matter-of-fact-ness that makes the images unsettling. They convey an uncanny resonance by revealing connections between some very ordinary contemporary locations, history and remembrance, as the street signs repeatedly name what's missing from all these places.

When I had completed my journey, it seemed to me as if those hundreds of signs made up a chorus calling out emphatically, over and over again, the name of what is gone forever.

A photographic image can only, ever, represent things as they are in the present moment when the image is 'taken'. But the present is a summation of everything that precedes it and each photograph will be seen in the context of everything that happens afterwards. In that way, *The J. Street Project* has allowed me to reflect not only on one unique, incurable, traumatic absence, but also on more recent attempts to destroy minority cultures and erase their presence.

Susan Hiller, 2005

Susan Hiller   *The J. Street Project (Film)*   2002–2005

Jerome

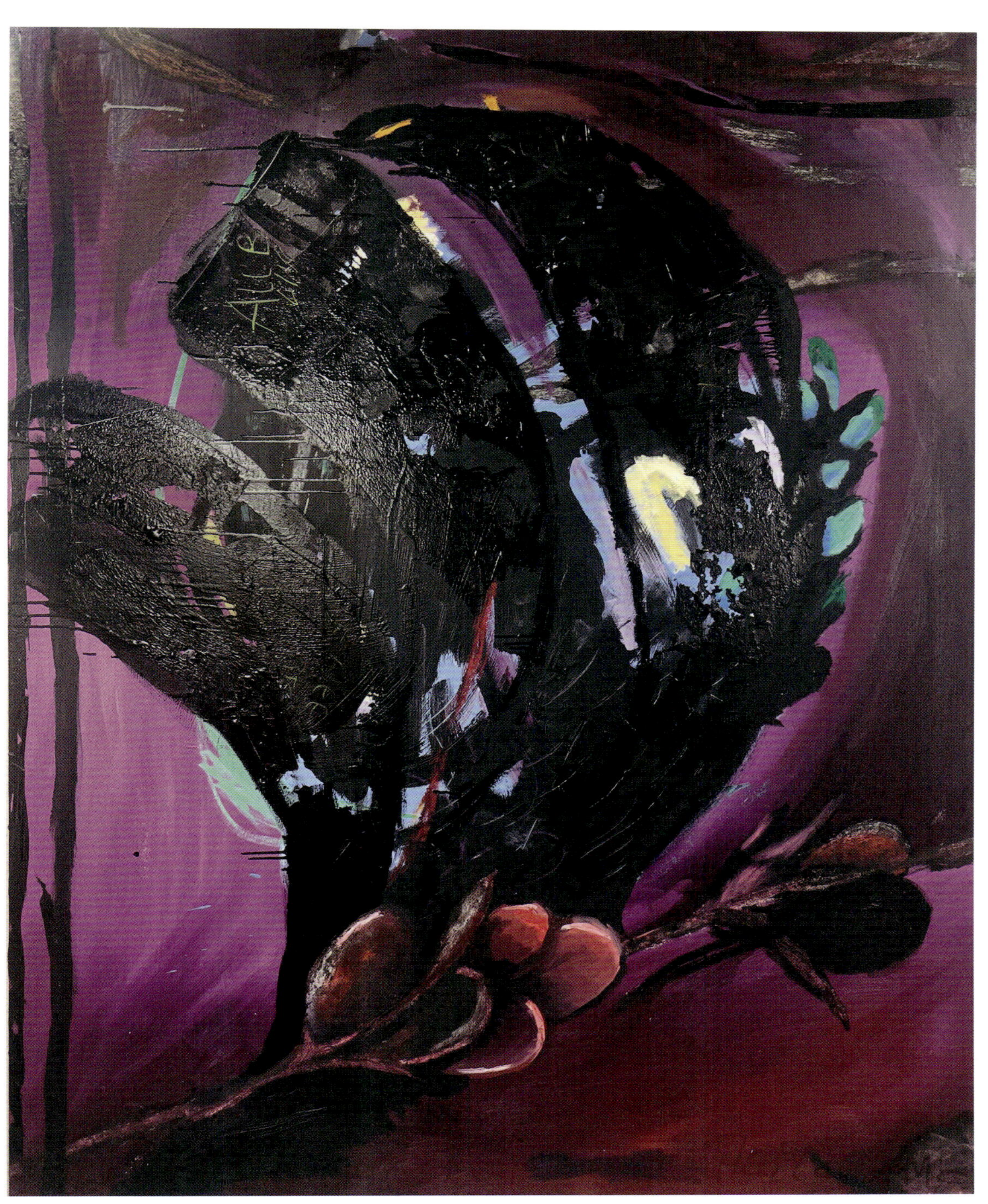

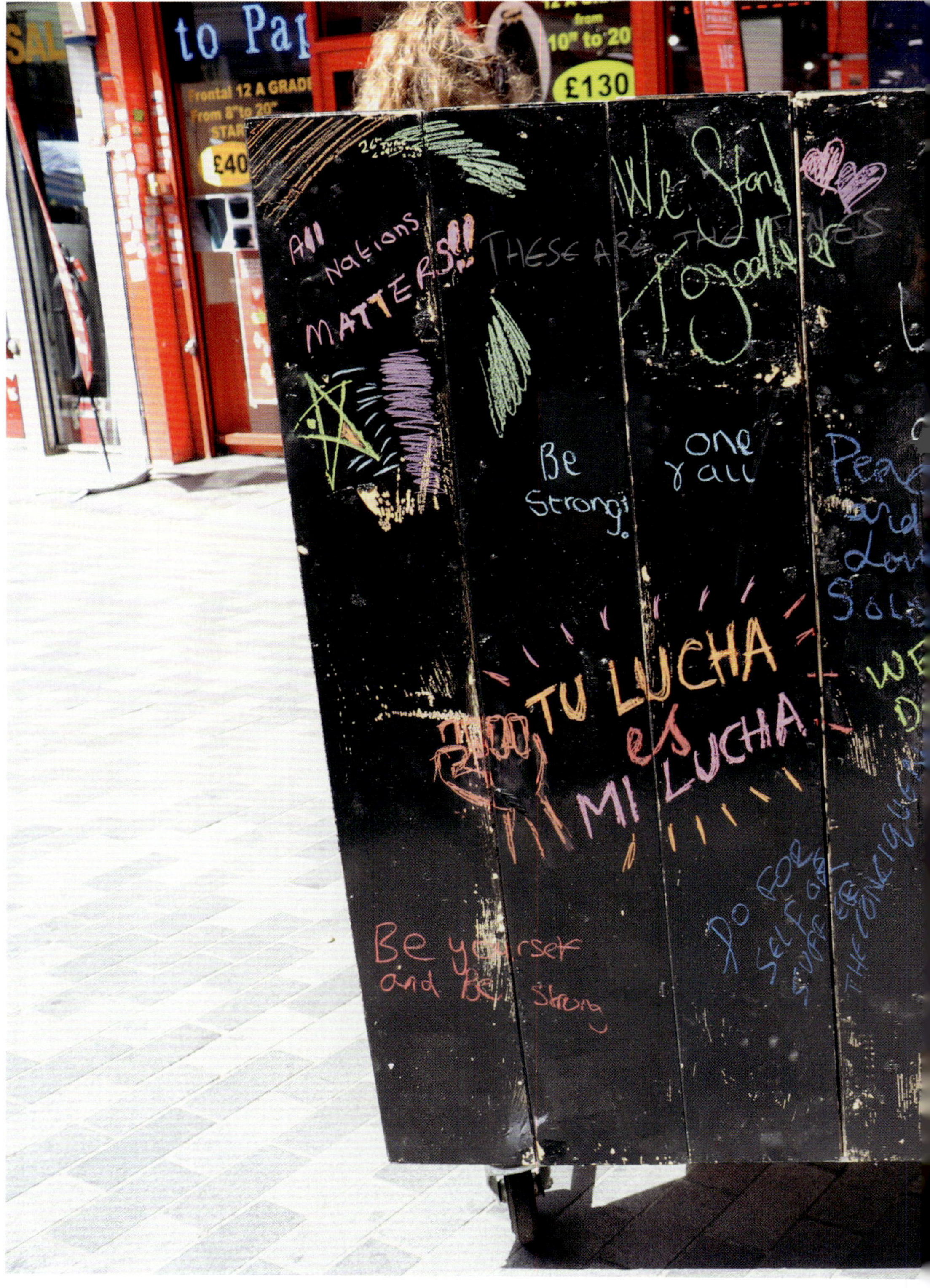
to Pap
£130
SAL
Frontal 12 A GRADE
From 8" to 20"
STAR
£40
All Nations MATTERS!!
THESE ARE THE
We Stand Together
Be Strong!
one y'all
Peace and Love Sols
TU LUCHA es MI LUCHA
WE
Be yourself and Be strong
DO FOR SELF OR SUFFER THE CONSEQUENCE

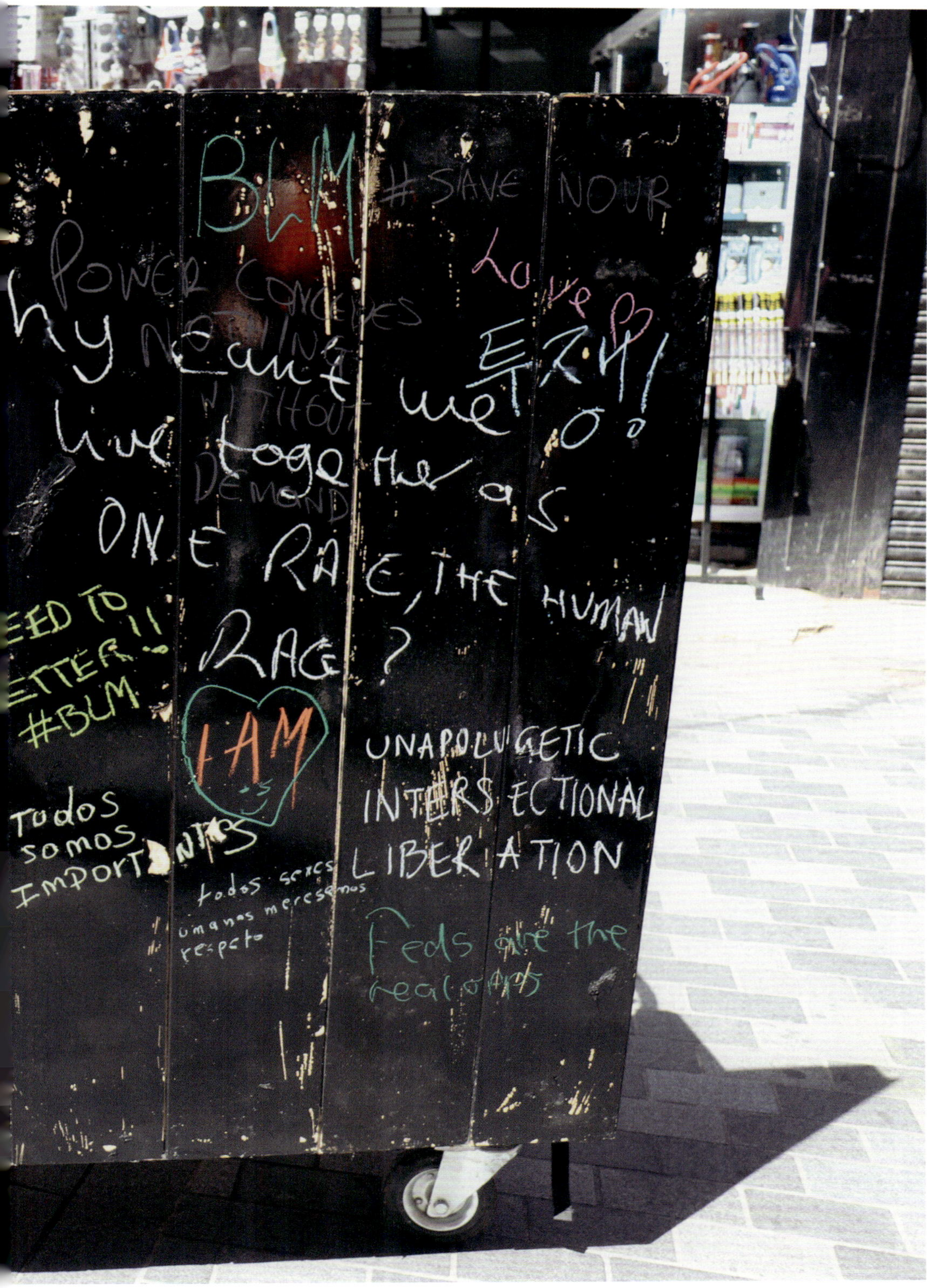
BLM
#SAVE NOUR
POWER CONCEDES
Love
hy ne an't
E.R.H!
live togethe as
ONE RAE,THE HUMAN
RAGE ?
EED TO!!
ETTER!
#BLM
I AM
UNAPOLOGETIC
INTERSECTIONAL
todos
somos
IMPORTANTS
LIBERATION
todos sencs
umanos merecemos
respeto
Feds are the
real cops

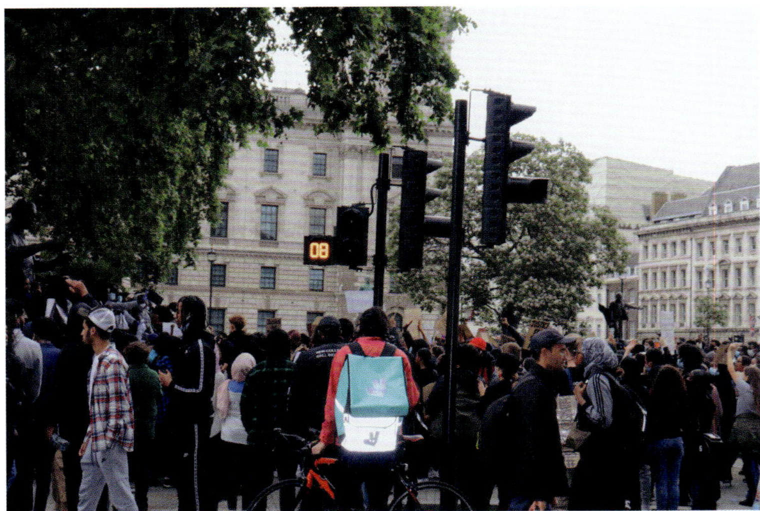

'Action Black' is the title for this body of work that explores how living moments can be captured and expressed through painting.

The black paint is initially applied to vinyl flooring during the pre-activation stage, which is the first of three different stages that can connect, overlap, and disconnect at multiple points. These stages can be described as pre-activation, activation, post-activation and re-activation, and form part of an ecological process that utilises the live dialogue between viewers, participants, artist, and paint in order to activate the work.

The vinyl flooring has been used in fashion shows, dinners, protests, musical experiences, and performances. During each event, viewers are invited to write in oil pastel what they are feeling at the time. The paint is later stripped from the floorboards and used as a medium within 'Action Black' paintings. The conversations present, within the works often result in interesting dialogues amongst strangers from considerably different entry points, and especially if the floorboards are reused in another event before being used within paintings.

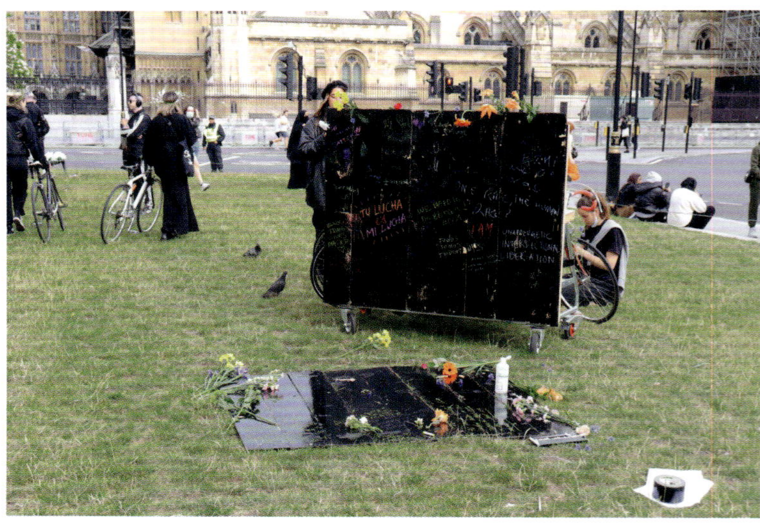

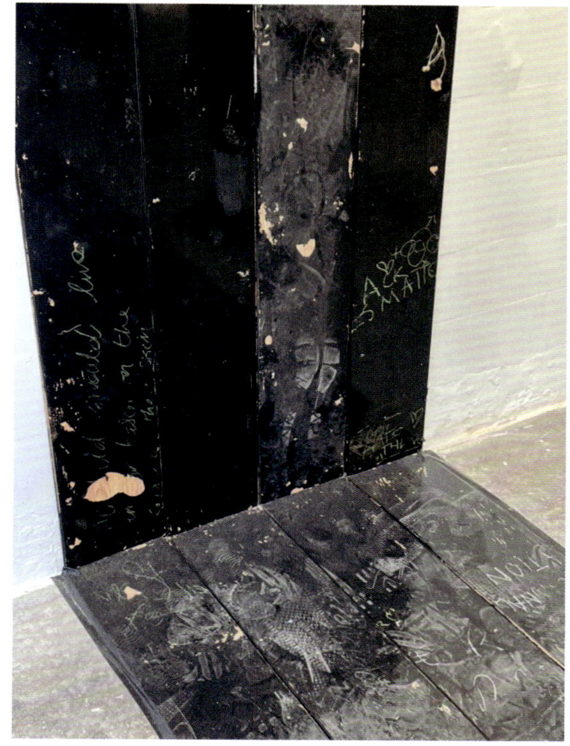

The works presented for the *Life is More Important than Art* exhibition allow viewers to see the work in two versions of the re-activation stage. The compositions within the paintings elaborate on conversations present in the works of Clyfford Still and Pierre Soulages but were initially begun as a response to missing the funeral of my late friend, Richmond Cloverfield; an artist and admirer of the 'Action Black' works. The floral compositions are an ode to Cloverfield's name as one of the last messages he sent me was asking to use the name Action Black in some way for his own works and the full title of this series is 'Action Black: Cloverfield'.

Jerome, 2023

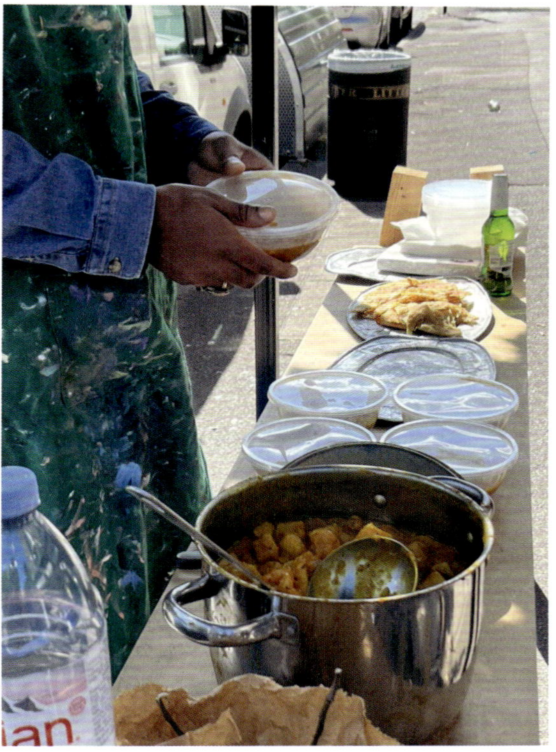

Matthew Krishanu

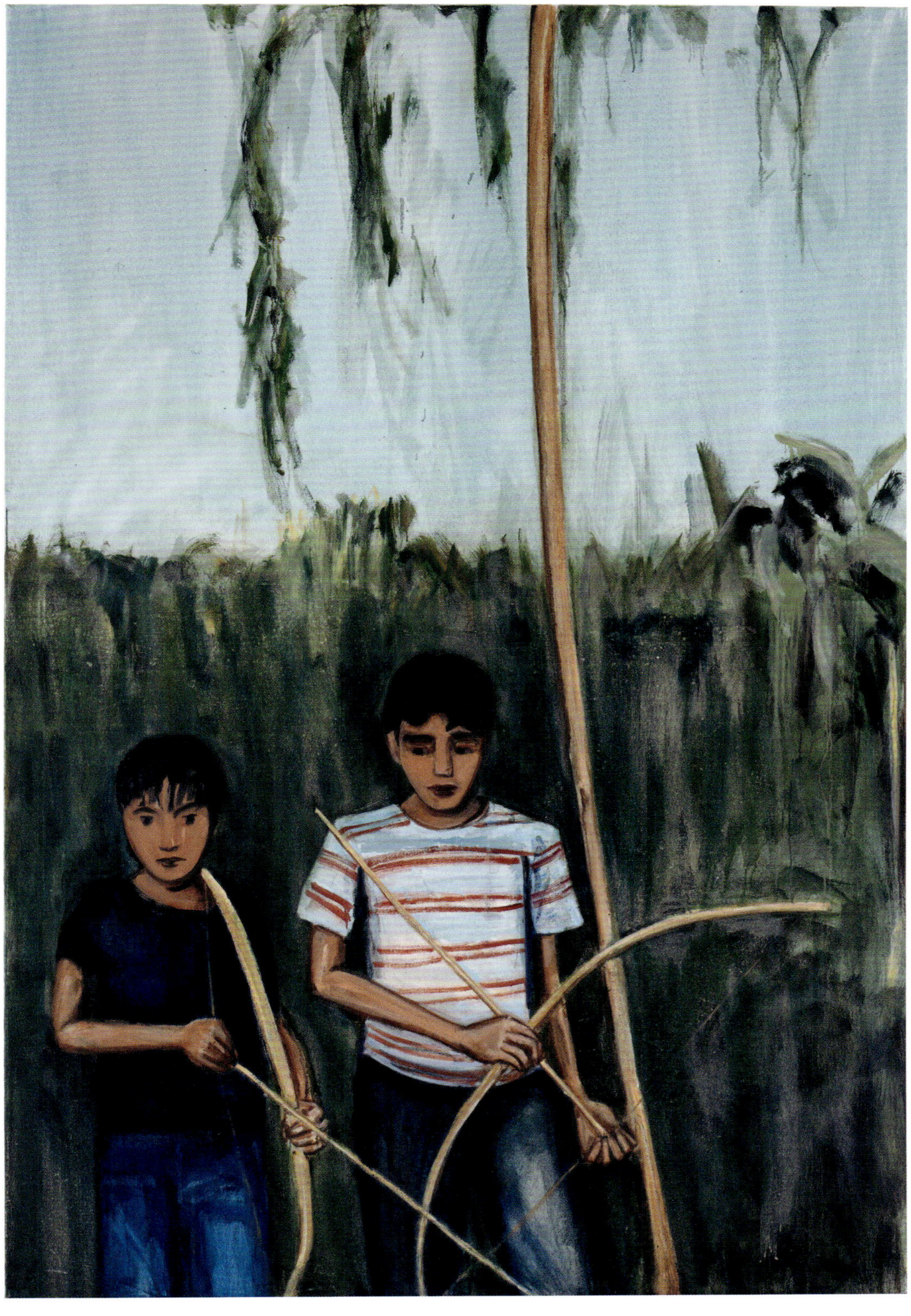

The painted world that I want to create, whether I'm addressing one single painting or an overall body of work, is something to do with being a thought-painting of different elements, with different weightings emotionally, that I feel in myself as I paint them: my emotional connection to the cross, my emotional connection to, say, the spade in the grave, or the feeding tube, or the person as a love object, or painting my father as a White man, as 'other'. More than memorialising – which sounds more totemic and more deliberate – I would say they are about processing something that has been experienced or understood that wants to take concrete form. With 'In Sickness and In Health', I saw turning to painting as a way of controlling the narrative of what was happening to us, which was completely outside of our control at that point, sadly – there was nothing we or the doctors could do any more. In order to survive – mentally, emotionally – your mind has to process. I had more time to look back over a longer period of decades when I was painting 'Another Country' or 'Mission', whereas I had to do the processing a lot more quickly when painting about Covid or in making the 'In Sickness and In Health' pieces. That's what separates out art as opposed to a commission or a well-built house [...] I can take something I do want to process and set about finding a visual form and language in order to achieve that.

Matthew Krishanu

Excerpt from 'The Puzzle of Painting; Matthew Krishanu interviewed by Ben Luke', *Matthew Krishanu*, Anomie Publishing, London, 2023

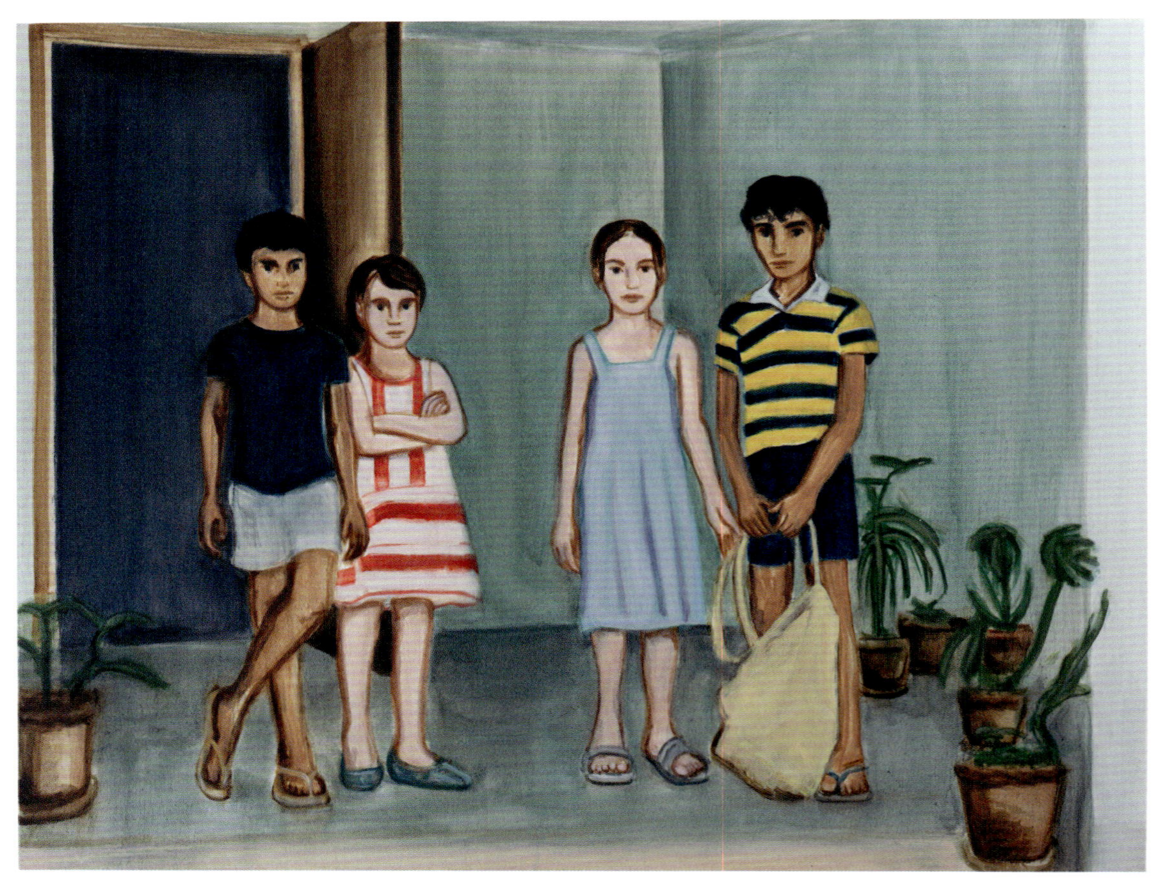

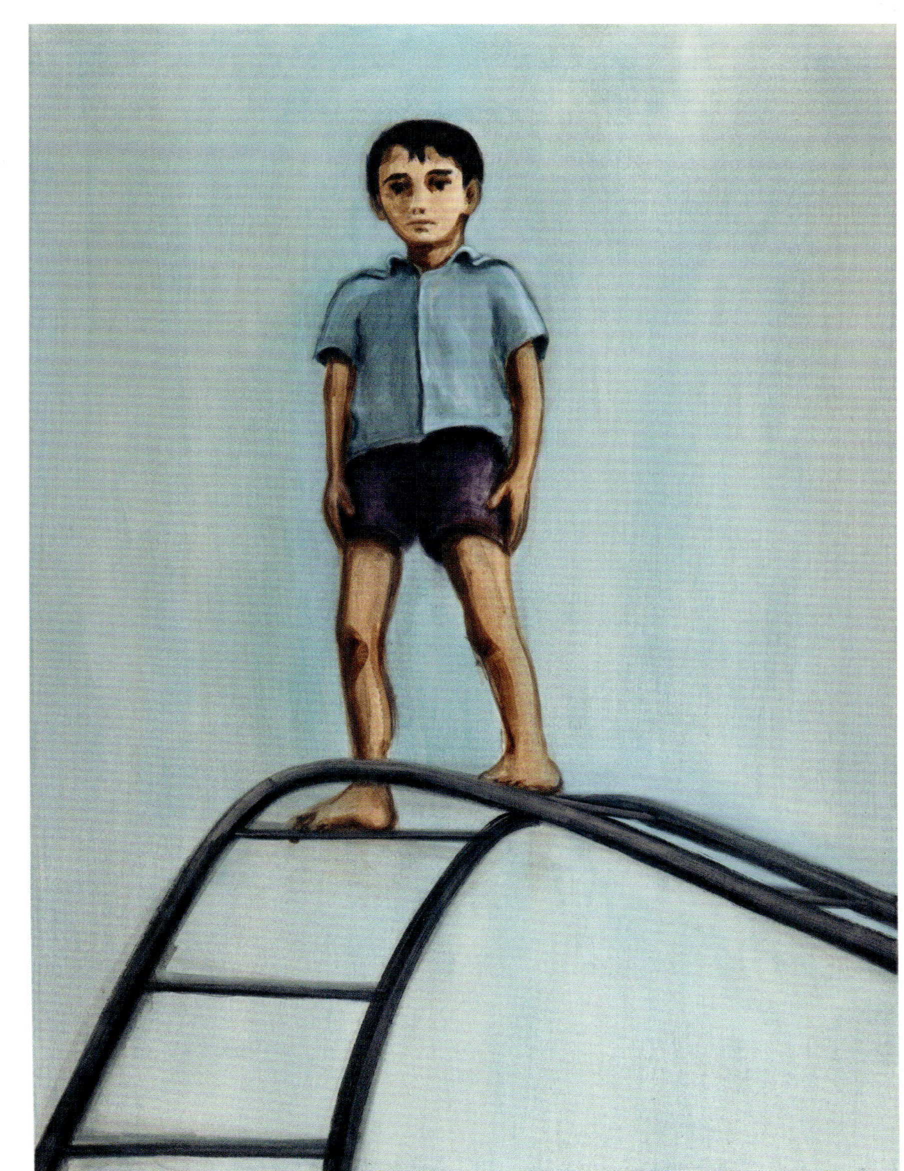

Page 47
Matthew Krishanu
Bows and Arrows
2018

Left
Matthew Krishanu
Four Children (Verandah)
2022

Right
Matthew Krishanu
Boy on a Climbing Frame
2022

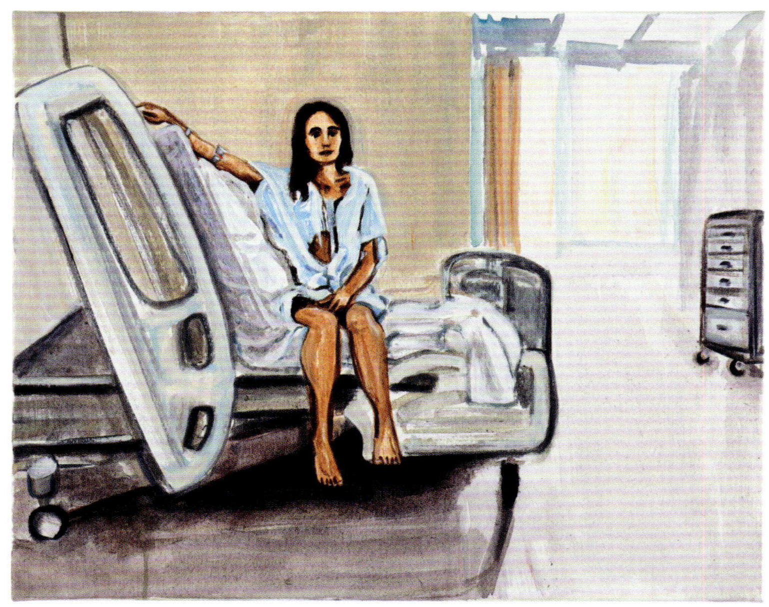

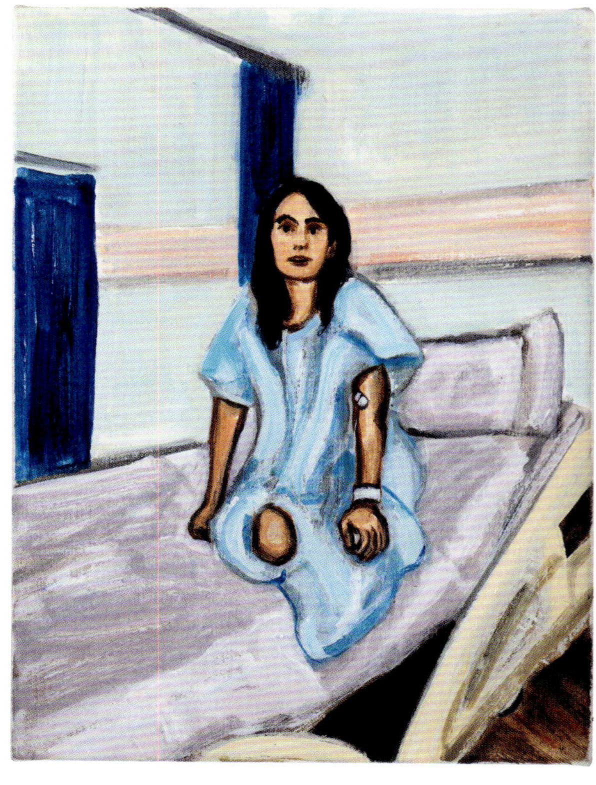

In Sickness and In Health (2007–2022)

Above
Matthew Krishanu
Hospital Bed (Barts)   2021

Right
Matthew Krishanu
Hospital Bed (Whipps Cross)   2021

Matthew Krishanu
The Convalescent (after Gwen John)   2022

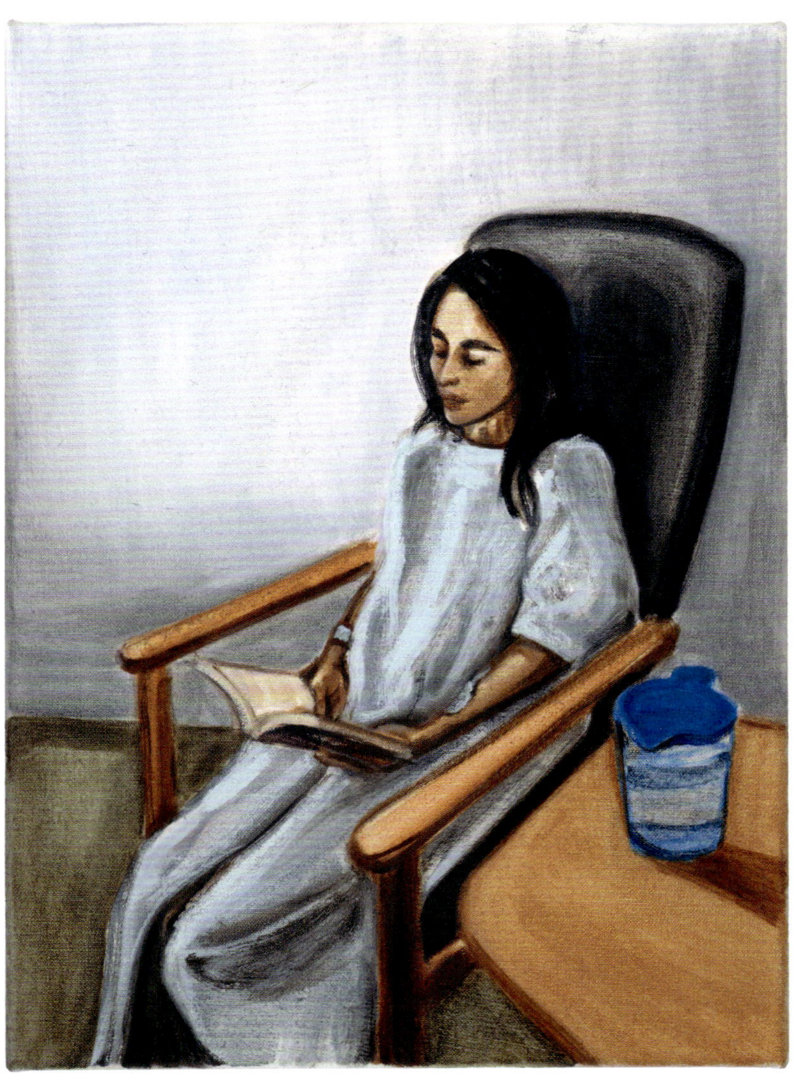

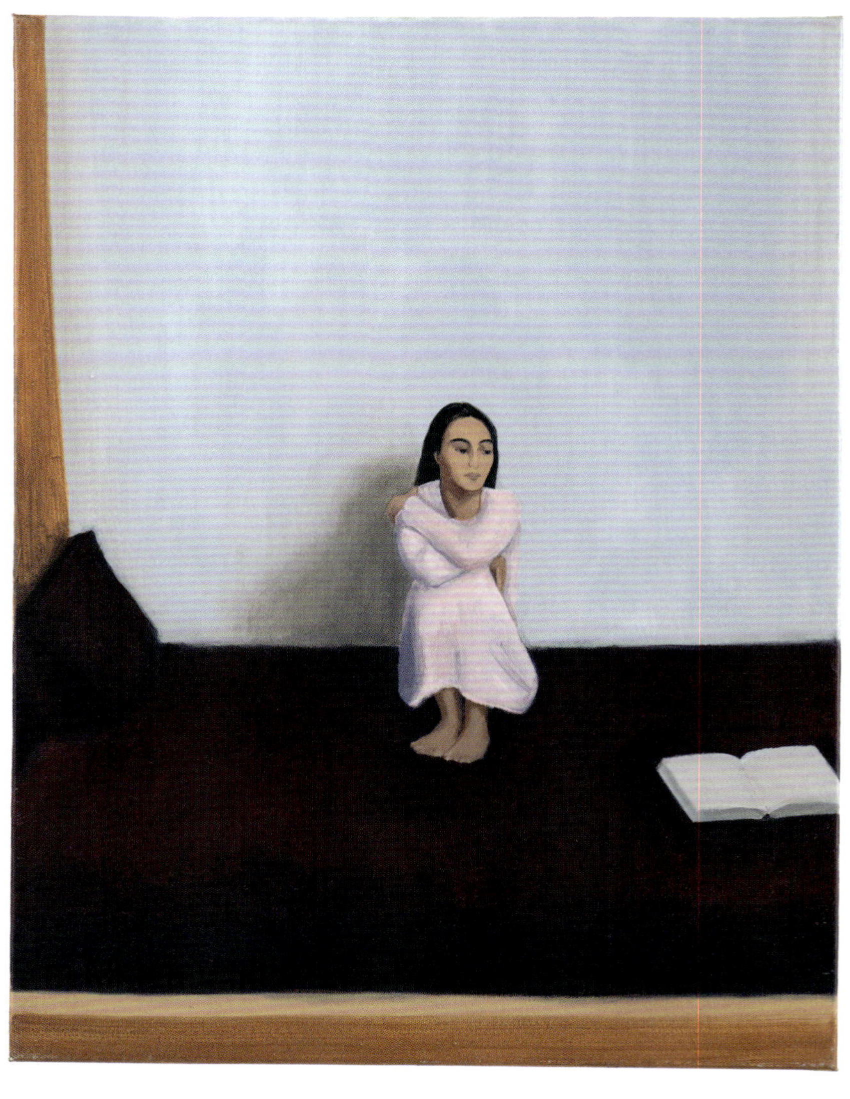

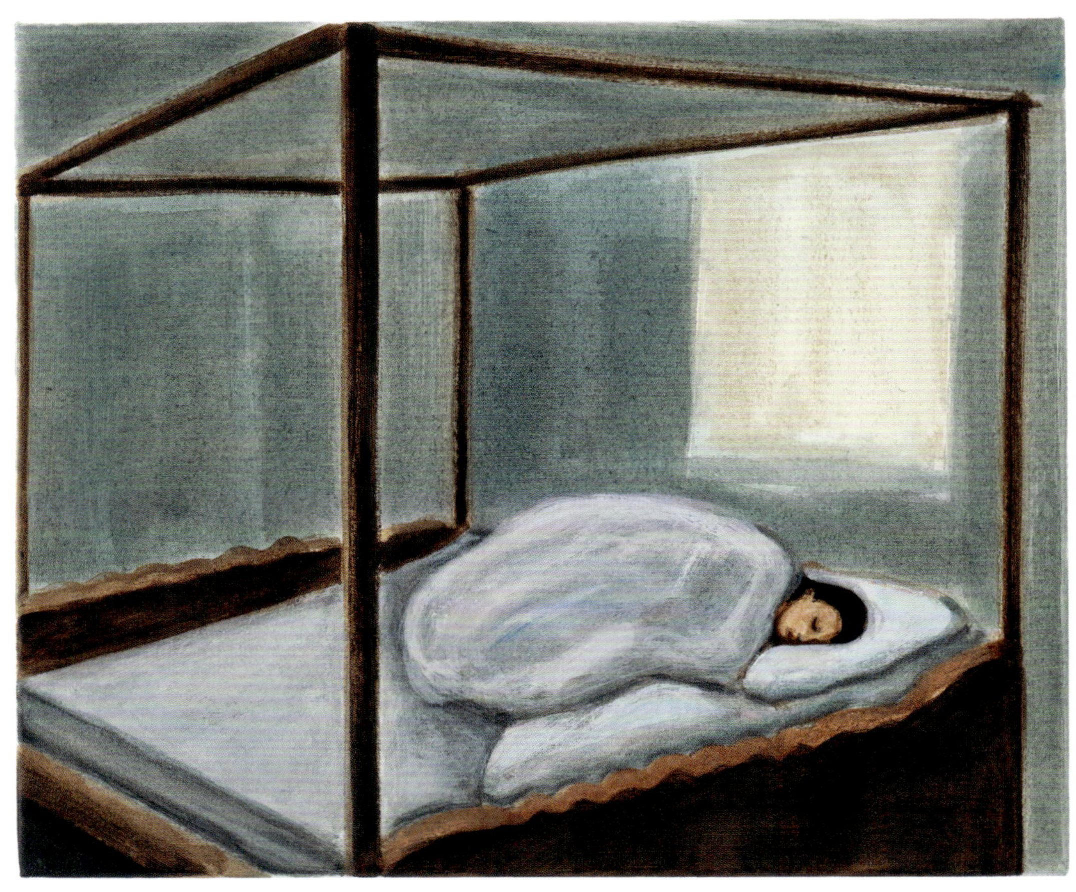

In Sickness and In Health (2007–2022)

Above
Matthew Krishanu
Four Poster Bed   2022

Left
Matthew Krishanu
Girl on a Bed   2007

Janette Parris

Janette Parris

THIS IS WHERE I WENT TO SEE *2001: A SPACE ODYSSEY* WHEN I WAS 16 WITH SOME FRIENDS. WE KEPT BEING TOLD TO BE QUIET AS WE WERE LOUDLY DISCUSSING HOW SHIT AND BORING WE ALL THOUGHT THE FILM WAS. IN FACT, WE LEFT BEFORE THE END. FAST FORWARD 20 YEARS LATER AND I NOW THINK IT'S ONE OF THE BEST FILMS EVER MADE. I'M NOT SURE THIS IS A GOOD THING, AS BECAUSE OF THIS I NOW STICK TO THE BITTER END WATCHING THE MOST AWFUL FILMS, JUST HOPING THEY WILL SUDDENLY TURN INTO MASTERPIECES. STANLEY KUBRICK HAS A LOT TO ANSWER FOR. MY MIND SAYS LIFE'S TOO SHORT AND I SHOULD LEAVE, BUT 'WHAT ABOUT *2001: A SPACE ODYSSEY*?', MY INNER VOICE CRIES.

There are lots of images of locations, sites and buildings that are not necessarily tourist attractions, so they're either shops, or local high street banks; I suppose the only famous one – which has been knocked down now – is the old West Ham football stadium, Upton Park. I did have an idea to write a musical, called *Closed*, about high street banks that are closing, or the changing high street, but even though I'm still doing that project, I decided to make this project a sort of graphic A to Z for East and South London. ...

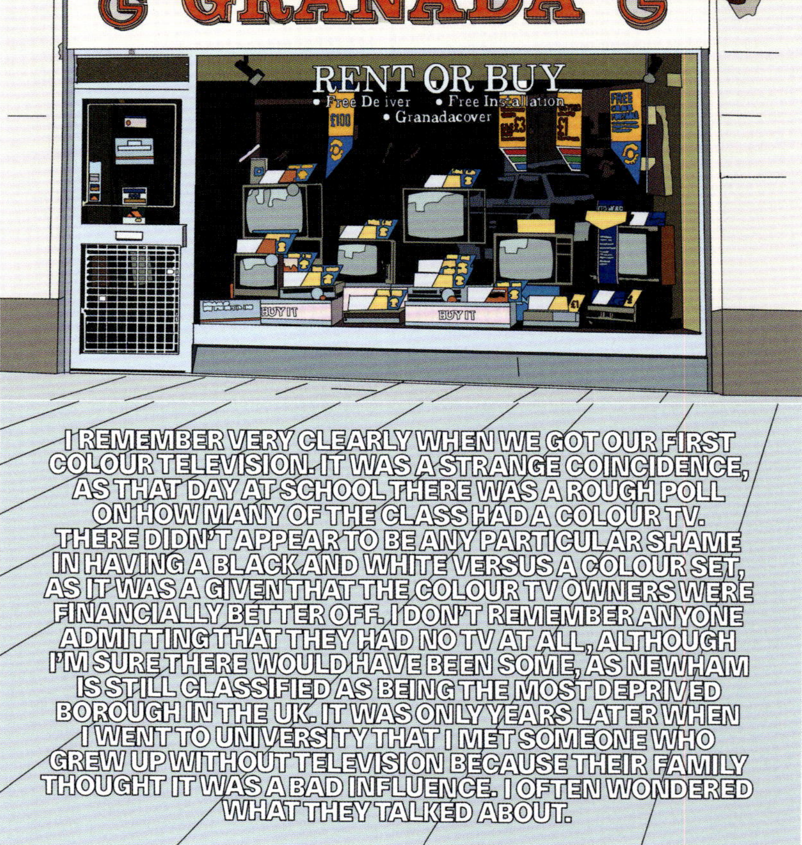

Page 55
Janette Parris
This is Not a Memoir
'Boleyn Cinema'   2023

Left
Janette Parris
This is Not a Memoir
'Granada TV'   2023

Right
Janette Parris
This is Not a Memoir
'Post Office'   2023

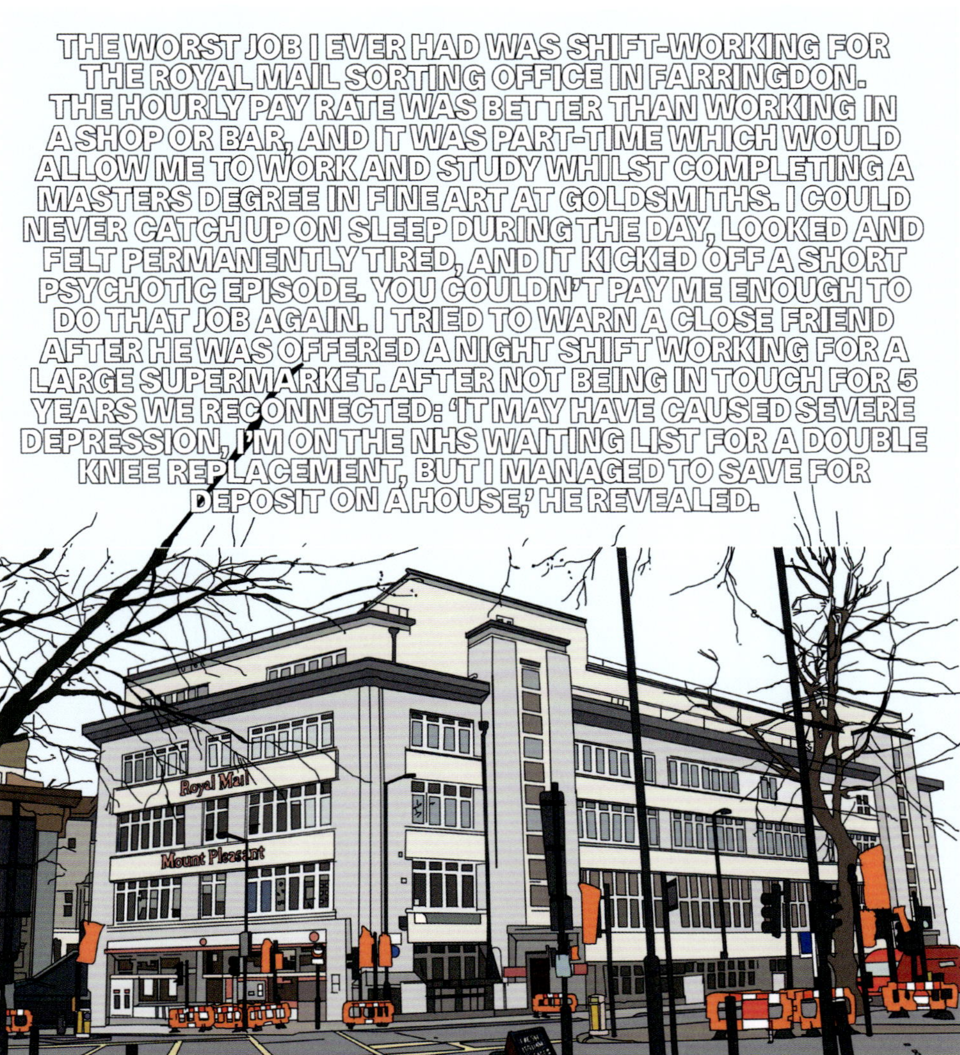

I don't know why I called the book *This Is Not A Memoir* because maybe I don't really like memoirs that much actually. It's only a moment in time and it's only what I've decided to focus on in that time so that's why it's not a memoir, you don't necessarily know everything about a person because they've written a memoir. I wanted it to be a slightly different type of memoir where you're not quite sure where the beginning is, you're not quite sure what the middle is, you're not quite sure where the end is.

And also, most people can relate to it in the sense that it's just sights around London, you know, they don't have to know me personally, they just know 'that's the old Ilford Palais'. Or 'that's the old Boleyn cinema', or something. It's a bit of an odd title for a book, you know, *This Is Not a Memoir,* but hey.

Janette Parris, 2023

Excerpt from 'Janette Parris in Conversation with Gilane Tawadros', *This is Not a Memoir,* Montez Press, London, 2023

John Smith

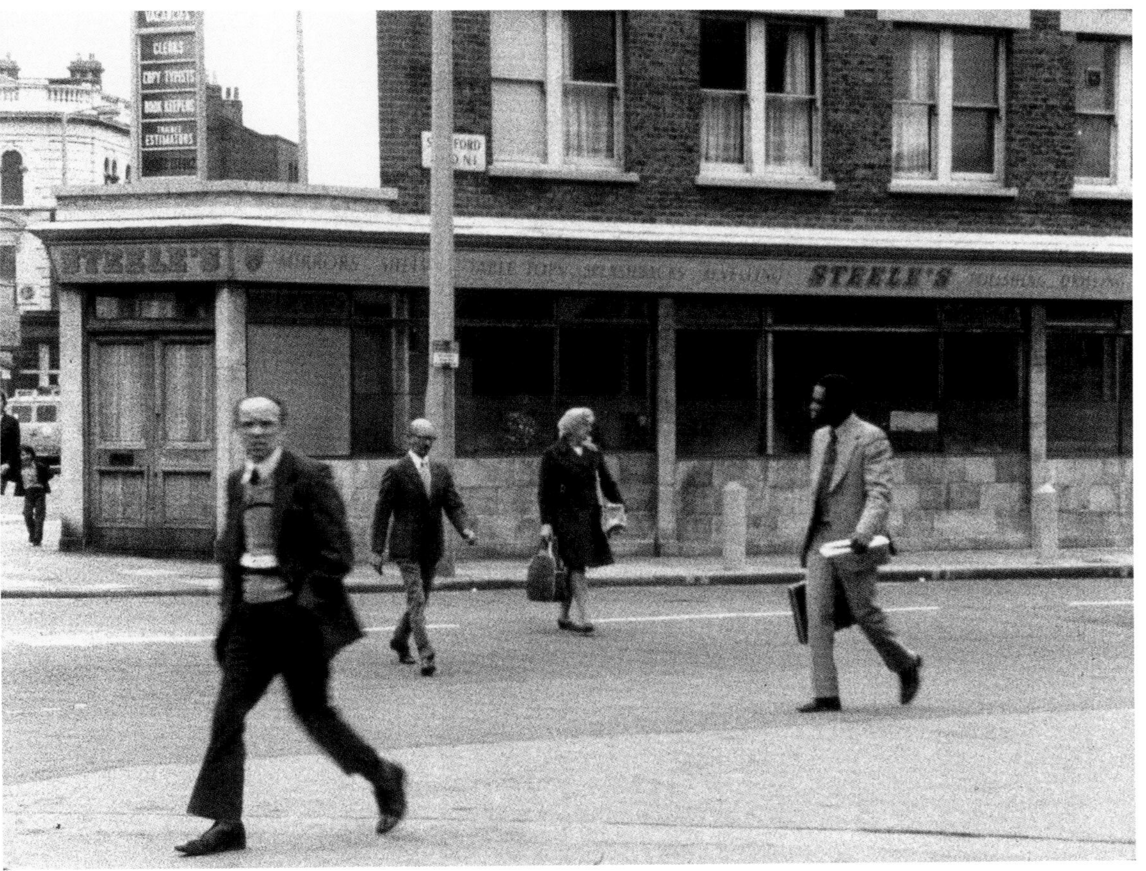
CLERKS
COPY TYPISTS
BOOK KEEPING
ESTIMATORS
STEELE'S
STEELE'S

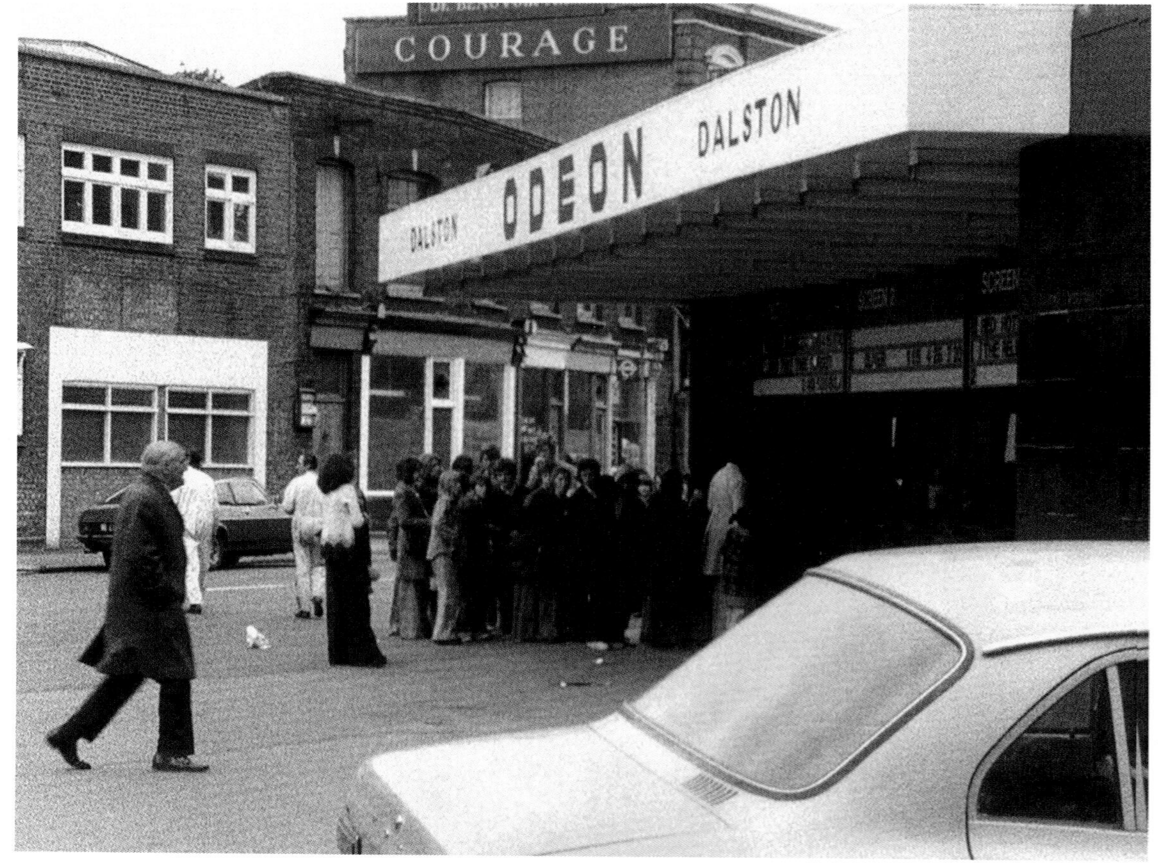
COURAGE
ODEON
DALSTON
DALSTON

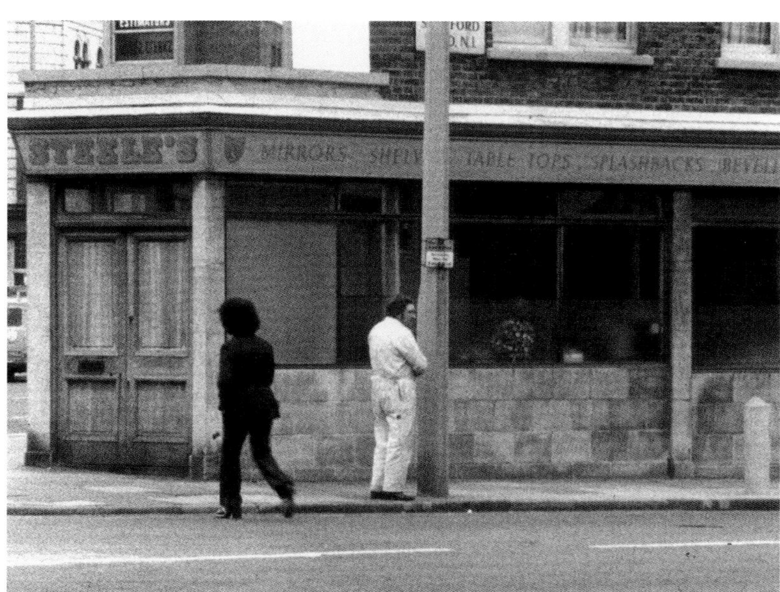

Pages 59–61
John Smith
The Girl Chewing Gum
1976

The Girl Chewing Gum was made in ideological opposition to the illusionism of mainstream cinema, at a time when many artists and filmmakers were creating films which sought to draw the viewer's attention to their material construction. Where most mainstream cinema attempts to make viewers identify with the actors in a story and forget that they are watching a film, myself and many others were making work which had the opposite ambition, to highlight cinema's inherent artifice. In a continuous shot showing everyday activity in a busy London street, *The Girl Chewing Gum* draws attention to the cinematic apparatus by denying its existence, treating representation as an absolute reality. The film achieves its ambition by using a voice-over to subvert the reading of the image, marking the beginnings of my ongoing love/hate relationship with the power of the word. Making *The Girl Chewing Gum* made me realise just how effectively the word can shape our perception of the world, a capacity that I've exploited in many of my subsequent films.

In 1976, as a 23-year-old art student, I never dreamt that my new film would still be watched by audiences in the 21st century. Although I have created more than 50 other films over the intervening years, *The Girl Chewing Gum* remains my best-known work. I have presented it personally on hundreds of occasions and it continues to be widely shown in museums, galleries, film festivals and independent cinemas, featuring in the syllabuses of universities, colleges and schools around the world. But over the 45 years since its debut it has gradually acquired an entirely new layer of meaning. When I devised the film I deliberately based it around the most ordinary present-day scenario, but 1976's mundane street scene has now become an almost exotic record of a distant time, where passers-by look like actors in period costumes, a difference made even more apparent by the ongoing gentrification of the film's East London location. To many young people the film looks like a relic from the early days of cinema, confirmed by school student blogs I have encountered which state that the black and white film, composed of only two shots, was made before colour film was invented, and before filmmakers learnt how to edit.

John Smith, 2022

Excerpt from artist statement on *The Girl Chewing Gum*, 2022

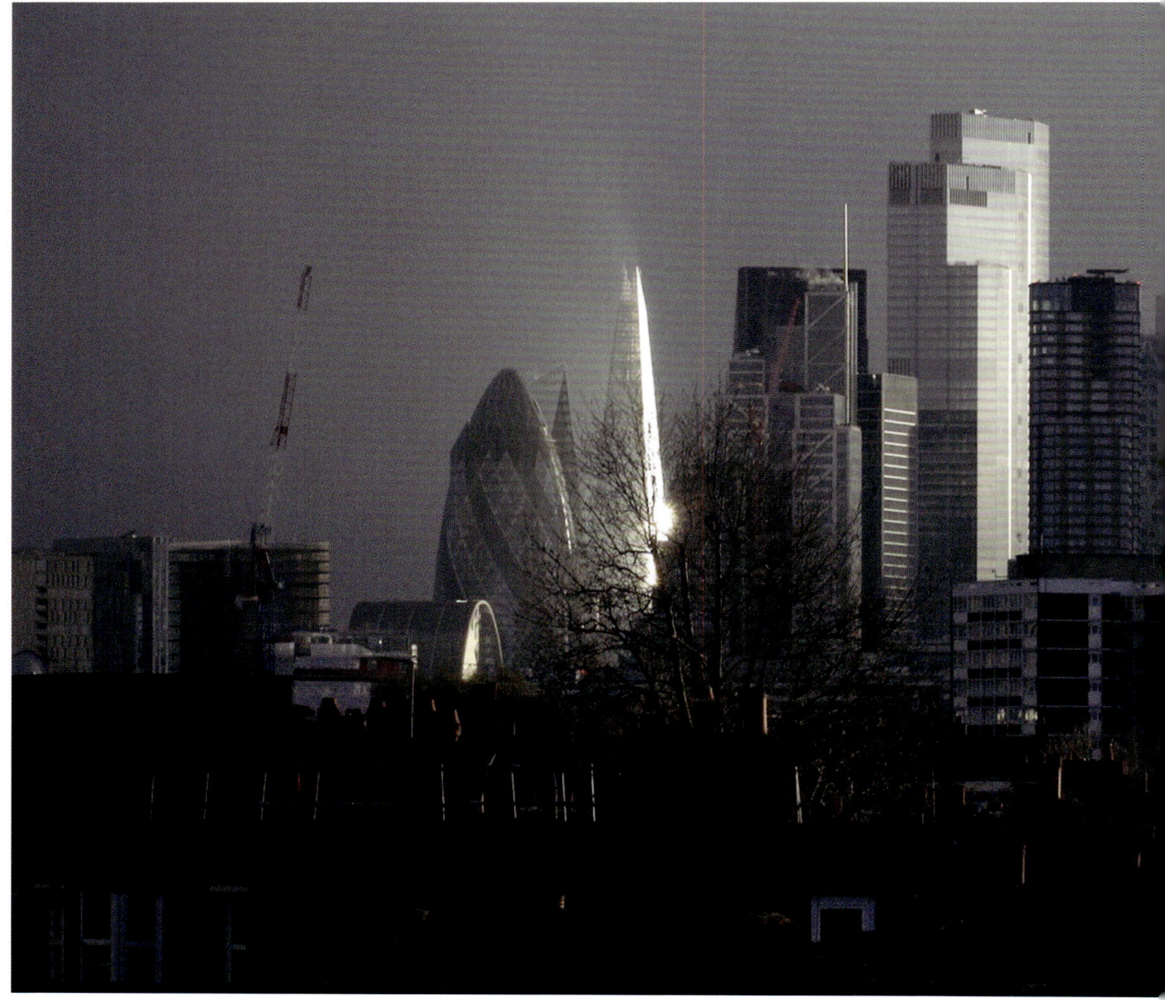

Although I only got around to it in 2020, I had planned to film the view from my bedroom window ever since I moved into my house in Hackney, east London, in 2003. At that time the distinctive 30 St Mary Axe building, better known as The Gherkin, had just been completed and was a central feature of the London skyline visible from my third floor vantage point. In those days The Gherkin was one of only a few tall buildings on the horizon, but in the intervening years the relentless expansion of the business centre of the City of London has resulted in a dense mass of skyscrapers that vie for attention, culminating in the colossal building at 22 Bishopsgate which has just been completed and now holds pride of place in the centre of my field of view. My desire to film this particular scene came out of observing the changes in light on the skyline in varying weather conditions at different times of day. Although the clutter of different architectural styles has now become an aesthetic mess, the effect of the ever-changing light on the heavily glazed buildings is highly dramatic and frequently mesmerising.

There was a reason for my lengthy procrastination. Although I had made numerous films in the past that were concerned primarily with the aesthetics of the image, this was something that I could no longer feel comfortable with. I couldn't look at the

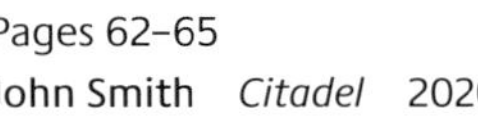

Pages 62–65
John Smith   *Citadel*   2020

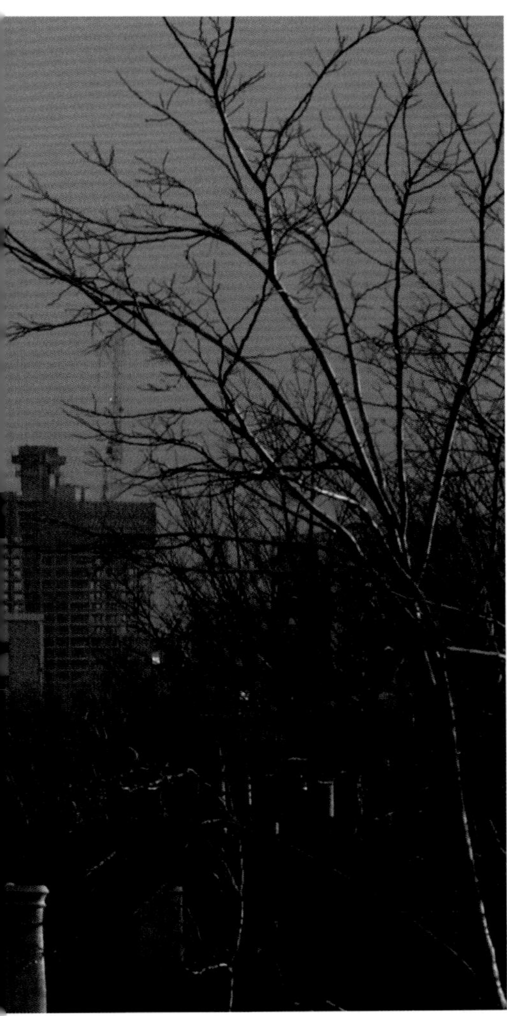

buildings of the City of London without thinking about what they represented, and without feeling a need to present them in a critical context. After Boris Johnson became Prime Minister in 2019 and formed a Tory cabinet that was even more ruthlessly business-driven than that of his predecessor Theresa May, I decided that I would start filming, with a vague idea of adding a spoken or written text to my images that would provide some kind of critique of neoliberalism. Then COVID-19 shook the world.

Suddenly everything fell into place and I knew that I had a clear starting point for my film. It became obvious very quickly that Johnson's Tory government was determined to place business interests before public health, initially seeing the spread of COVID-19 primarily as a business opportunity. I decided that I would combine excerpts from Johnson's speeches with my images of the city, filmically relocating the centre of power from Parliament to the financial district of the City of London, simultaneously presenting the city as a site of horror and visual pleasure.

Citadel was commissioned and produced by steirischer herbst '20, Graz, Austria.

Excerpt from artist statement, first published on mubi.com, January 2021

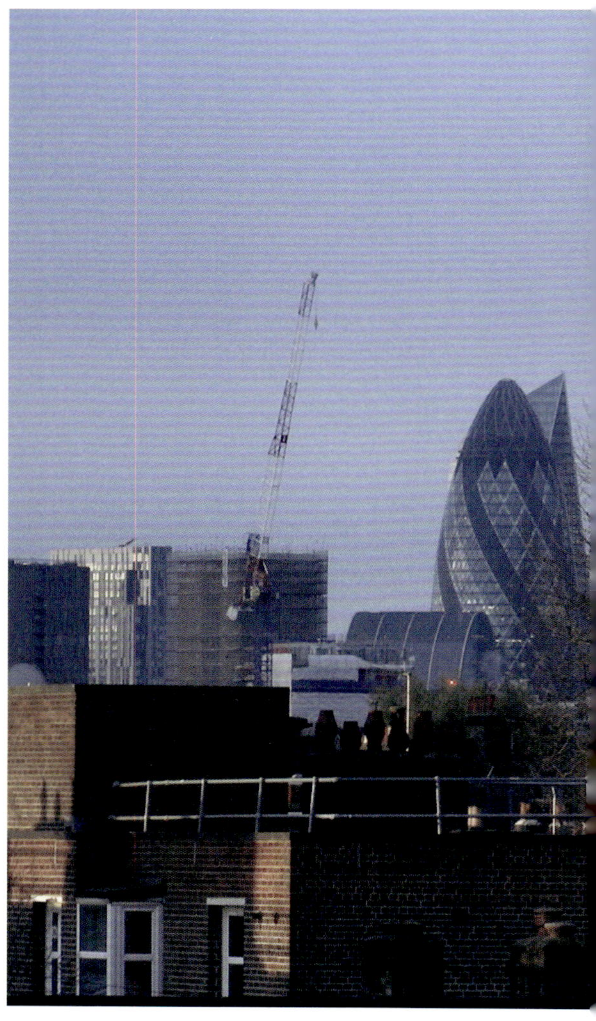

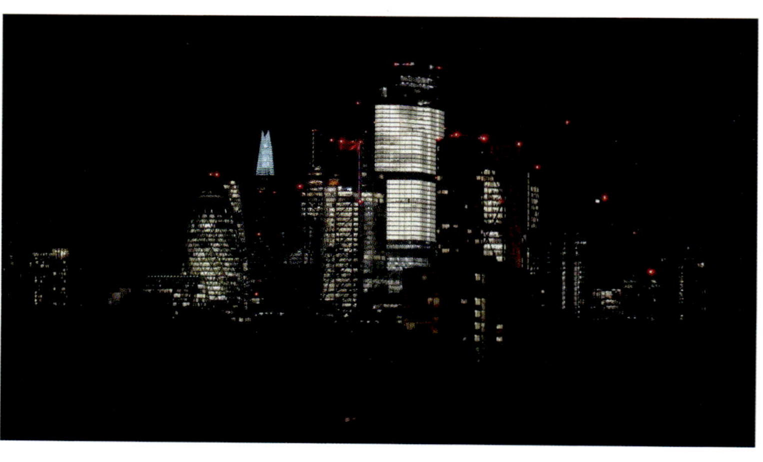

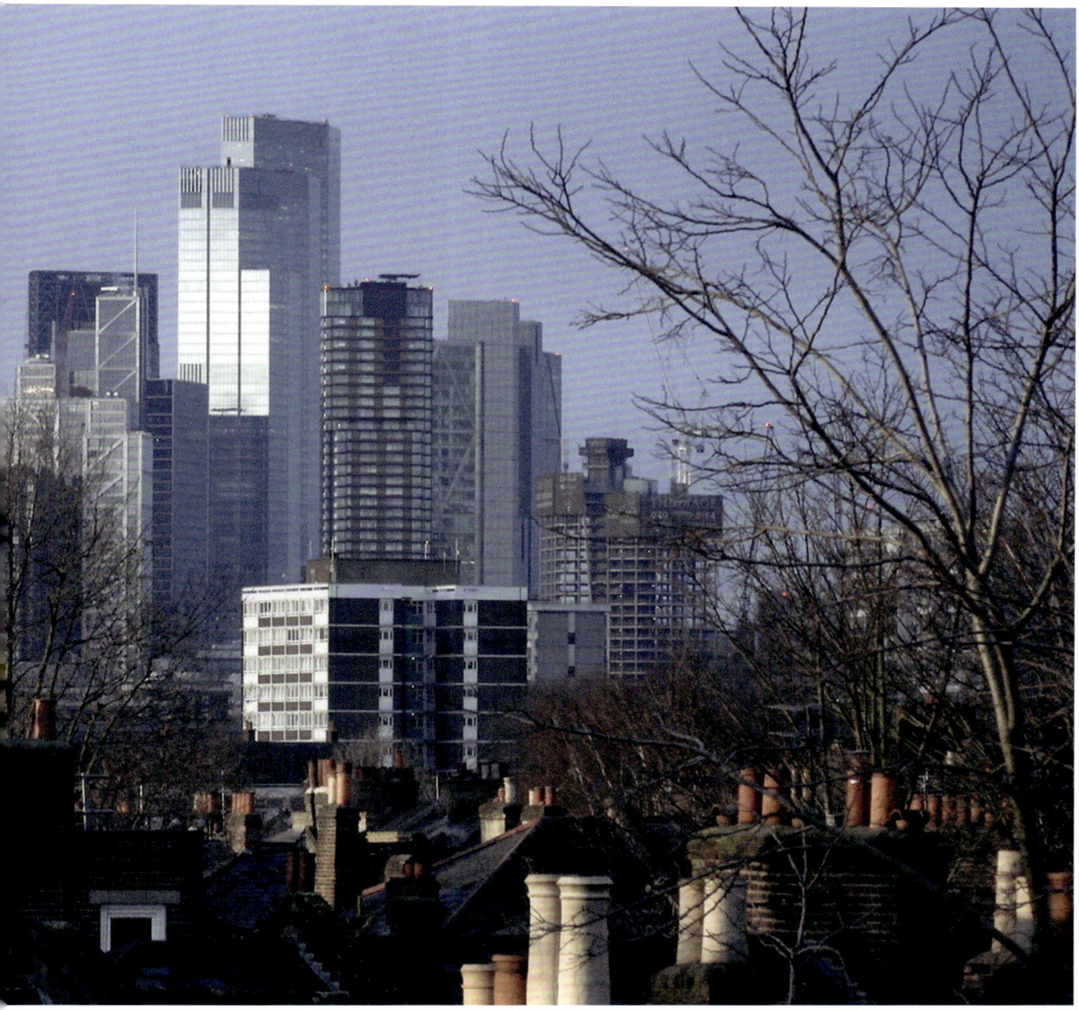

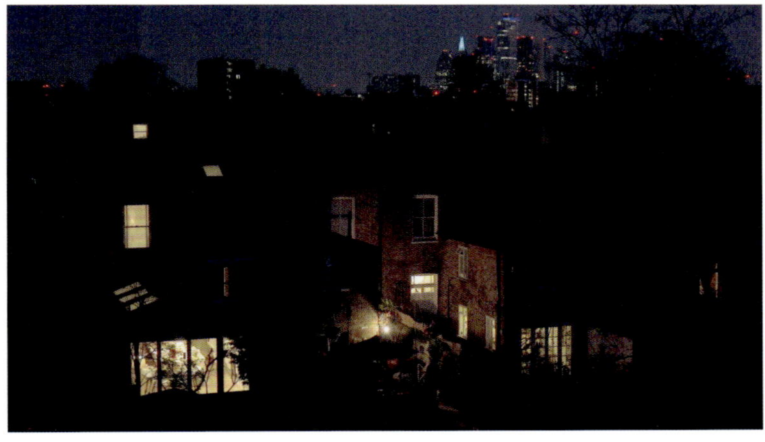

Alia Syed

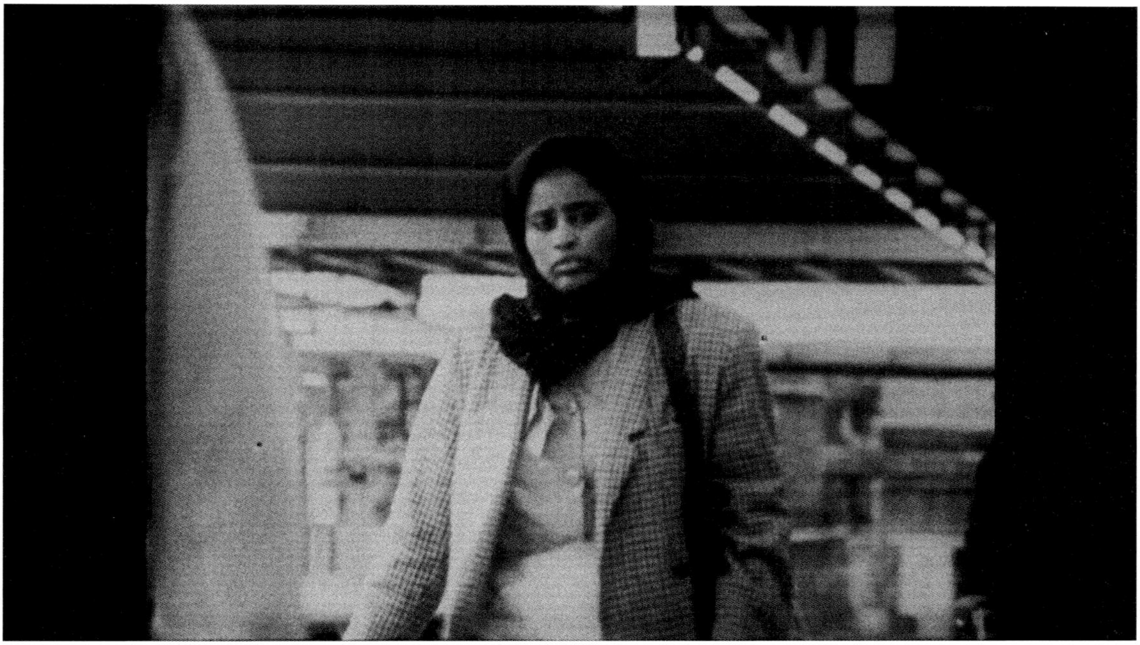

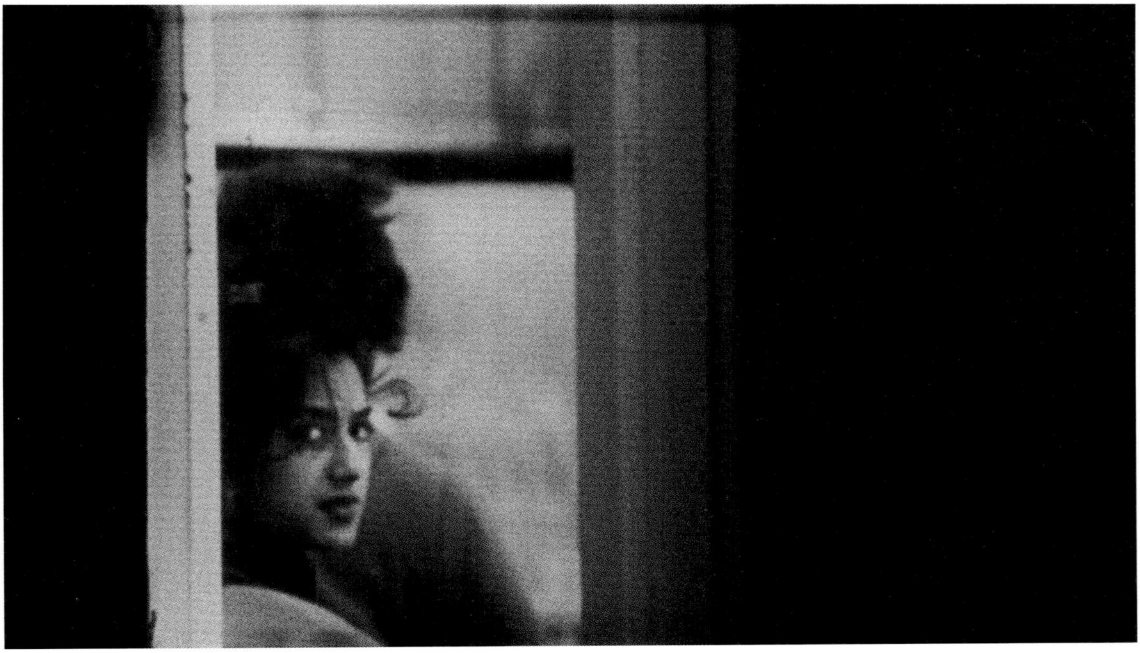

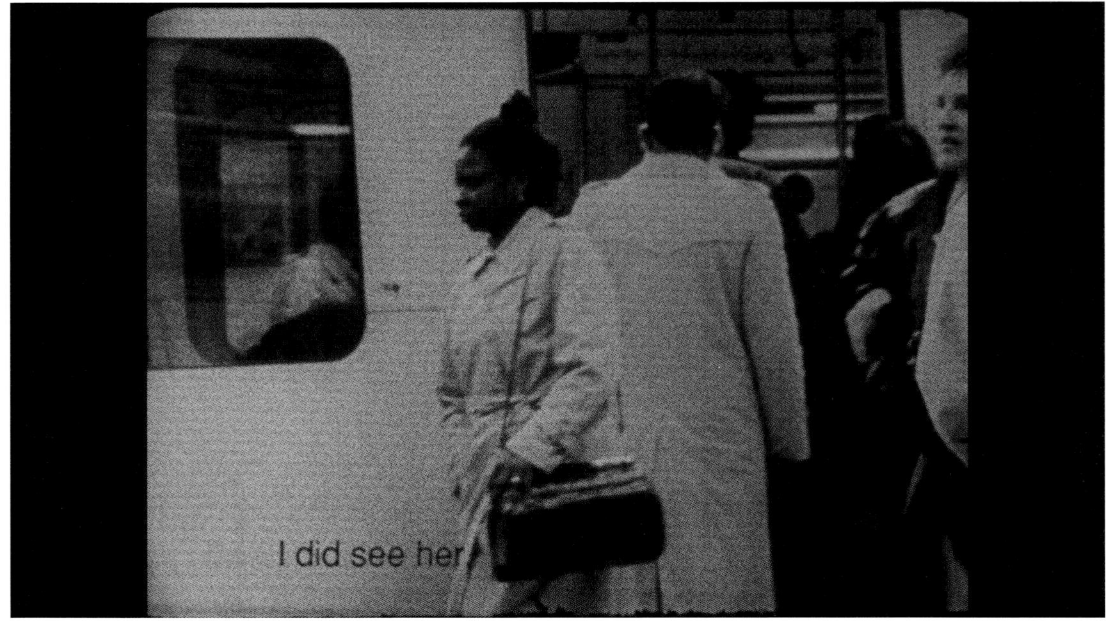

The surface of truth slips
Tongue licked and golden
A moment of childhood lost in the bleakness of facts

From New Cross Gate to Hoxton, seamless, the journey allows me to be
somewhere else. Faces take on significance. London has to be traversed
across. Recognition comes in bullets. External events collide – in my head –
a moment of clarity. I devote time to travelling. We look through siphons,
our attempts at observation are attempts to connect. Making becomes an
endless process of re-looking, of trying to find meaning – a point where I locate.

London is never London but contains traces of other cities, the poignancy of
the landscape lies in its ability to conjure, the sound of a horn, Karachi – one
city falls into another. Film time slips – formal tensions reflect more accurately
than actuality – a train approaches the platform, the sound quakes – they have
bombed another building – the folds of her dress move with the rapidity of
falling concrete – nine more children dead – dust – the slabs are too big for them.

An empty space.

The near is nearest when it speaks of
more than it is – intimacy
looking at the sunlight passing over the arm of the settee
footsteps running, children laughing
Butterflies only last momentarily
and catching them is difficult.
I look to recognise.

Pages 67–71
Alia Syed
Fatima's Letter
1992

'But in the daydream itself, the recollection of moments of confined, simple, shut in space are experiences of heart-warming space, of a space that does not seek to become extended, but would like above all still to be possessed.'[1]

Elements of displacement take place in recreating the daydream – not only in making the private public, in re-interpreting/presenting but also in the desire to remain possessed. "The source" no longer holds true – butterflies die and only the imprint of their wings remains, the breeze of their caress, gone. My memory is not yours. The butterfly reminded me, so I caught her. The memories become stories that I give to you. Stories travel on crests – quivering – wings regain flight. The nearest are always stories, allegory is the first form of documentary, inherited histories that in their telling soothe anxieties of loss from one generation to another. The best are expanded, one gesture holding the secret to so many unspoken clues, keys explaining the madness of generations, a blueprint that explains the unexplainable.

She writes a letter to Fatima, she speaks of her displacement, tells a story

In *Fatima's Letter* we position ourselves in relation to the languages within the film, various discontinuities in narrative, sound and image produce ruptures, different languages vie for authority – written over spoken – image over text – word image over documentary footage. We become part of a dialogue, we see ourselves within ideology. The static film frame becomes a stage. We become an audience to ourselves.

1 Gaston Bachelard, *The Poetics of Space* (Boston: Beacon Press, 1994).

Alia Syed, 'From New Cross Gate to Hoxton', originally published by *art in-sight* on the occasion of Alia Syed's retrospective screening at Brief Encounters in Bristol on 22 November 2002, *Alia Syed: Imprints, Documents, Fictions*, Courtisane, Ghent 2023

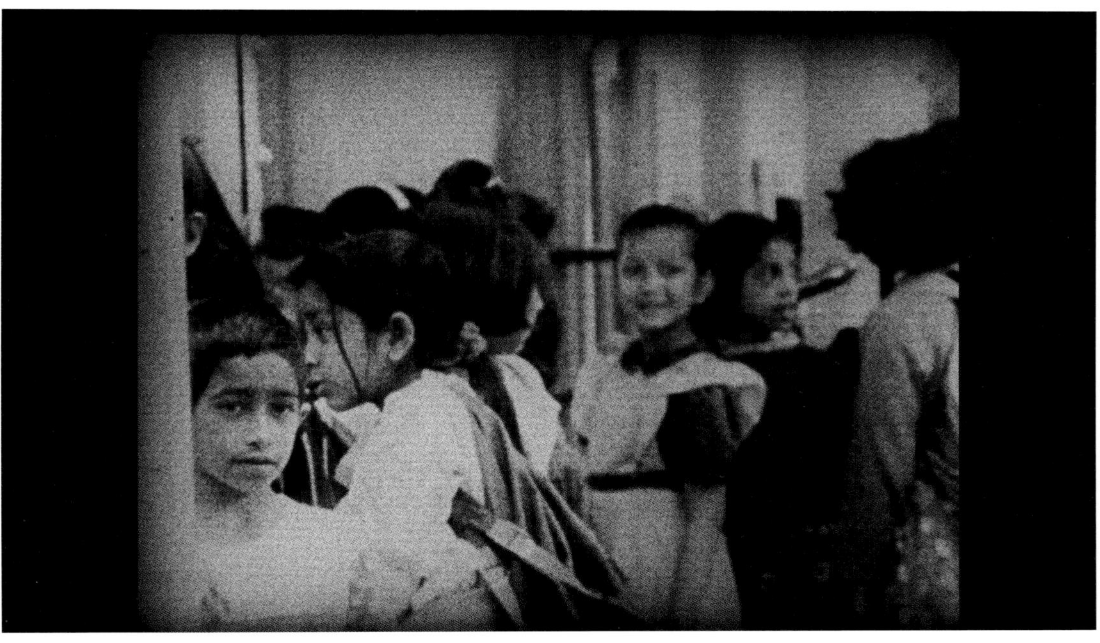

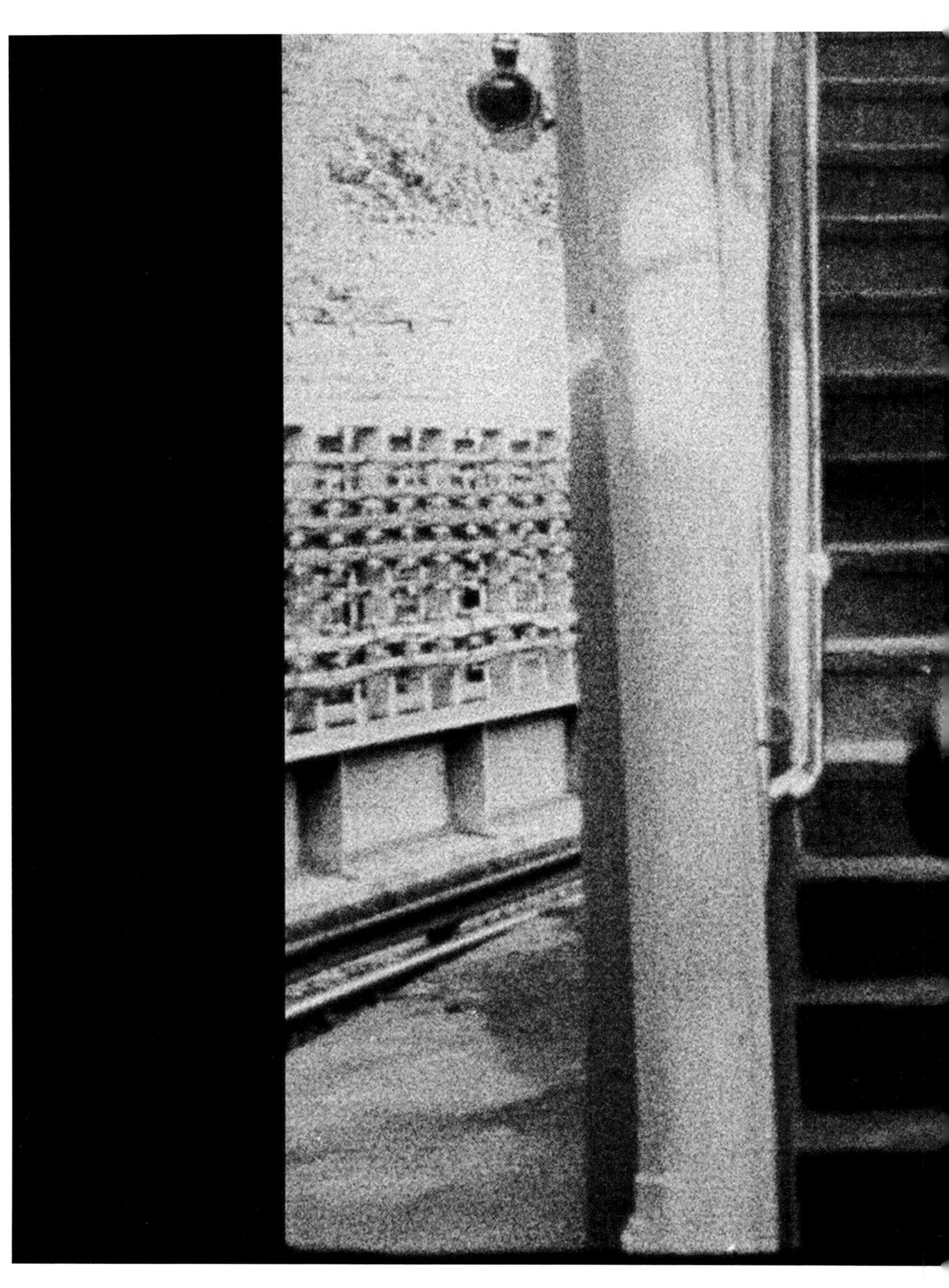

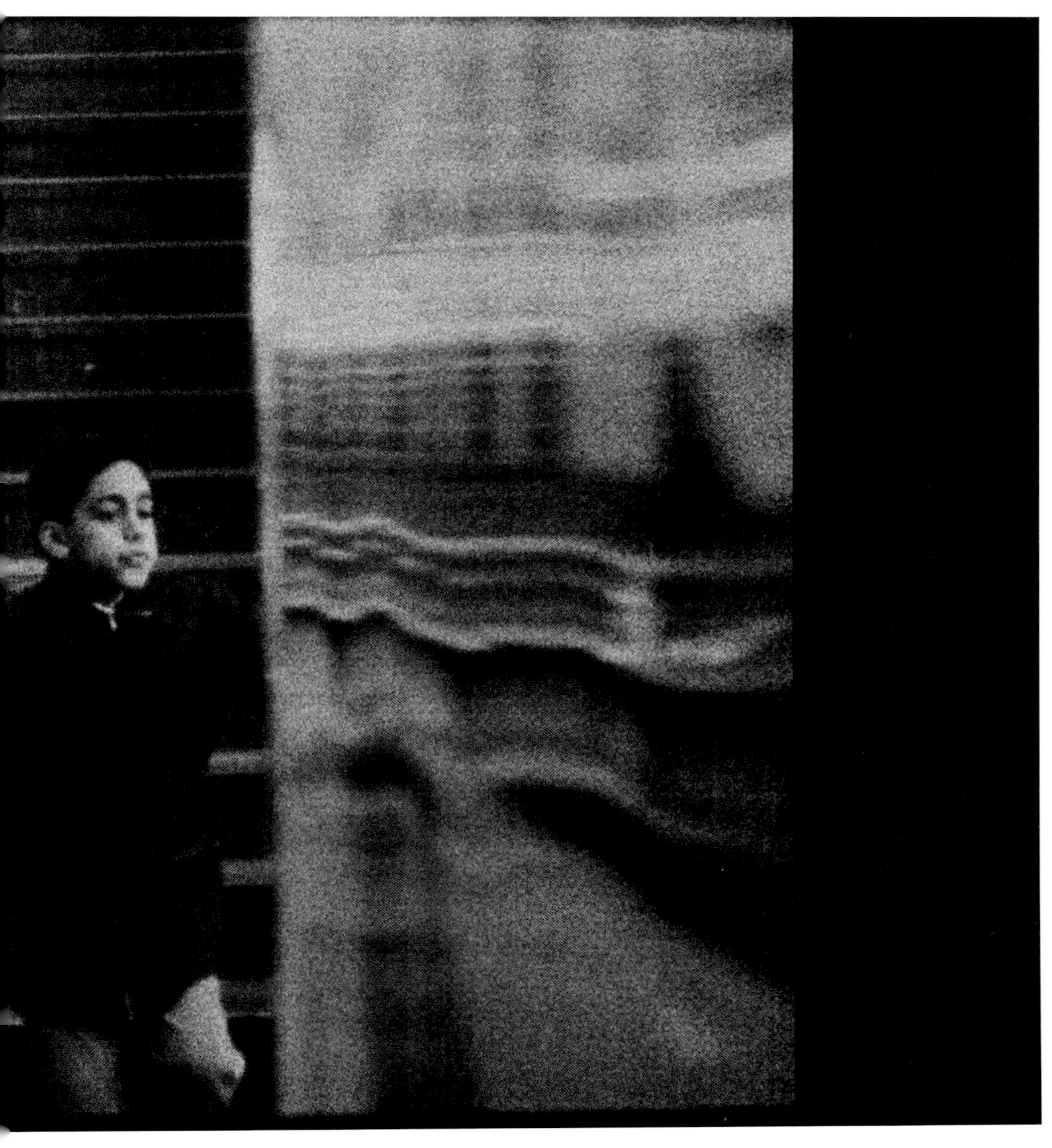

Mitra Tabrizian

Mitra Tabrizian

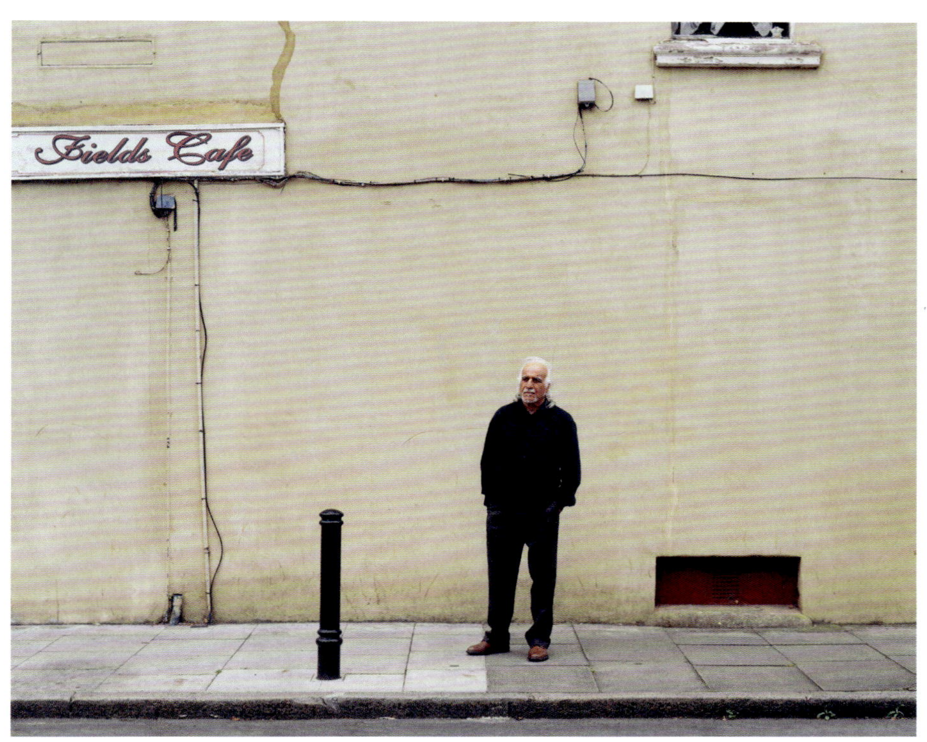

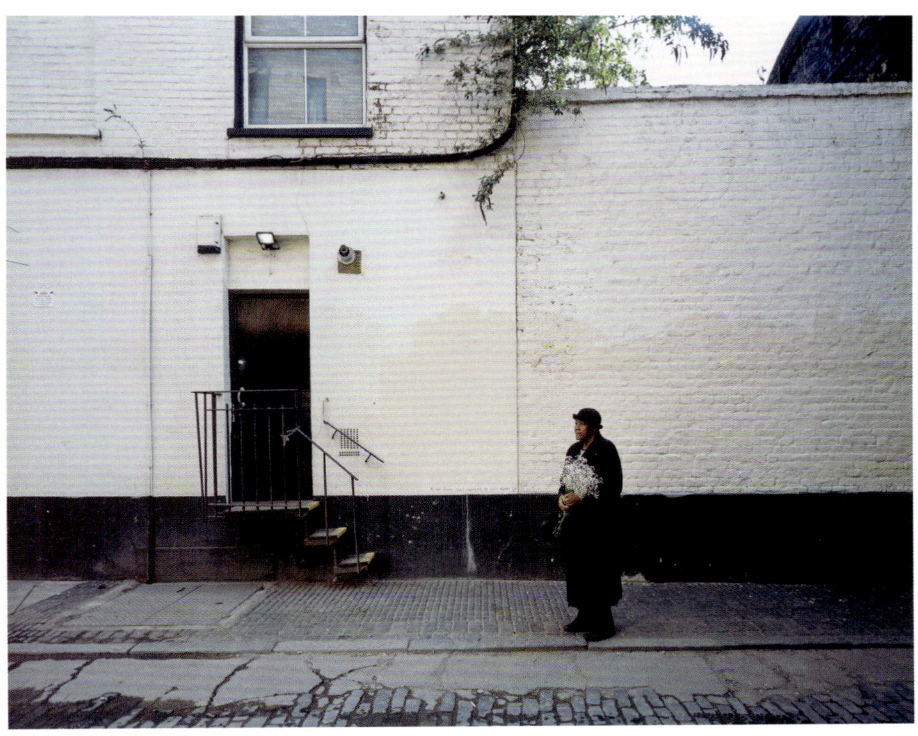

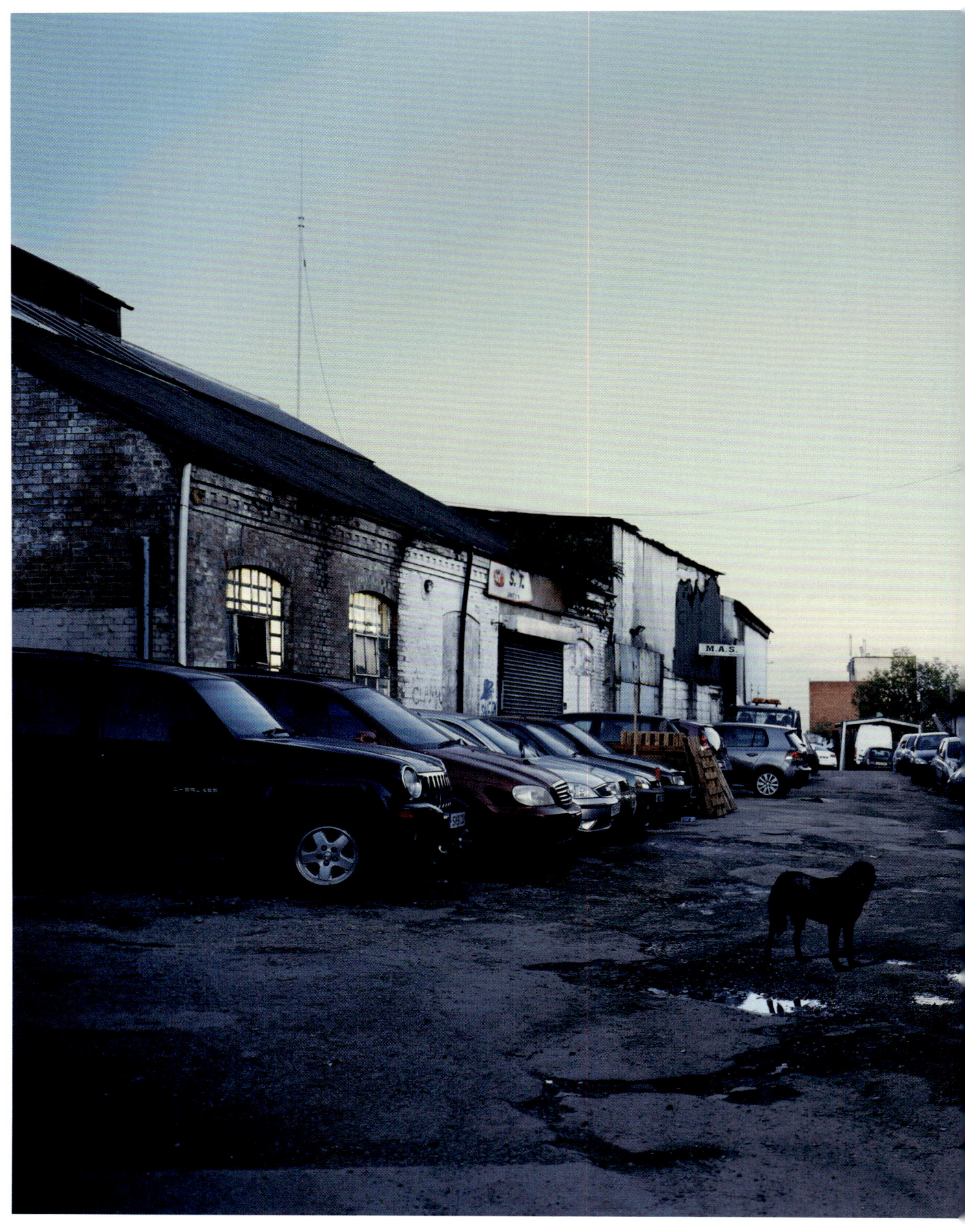

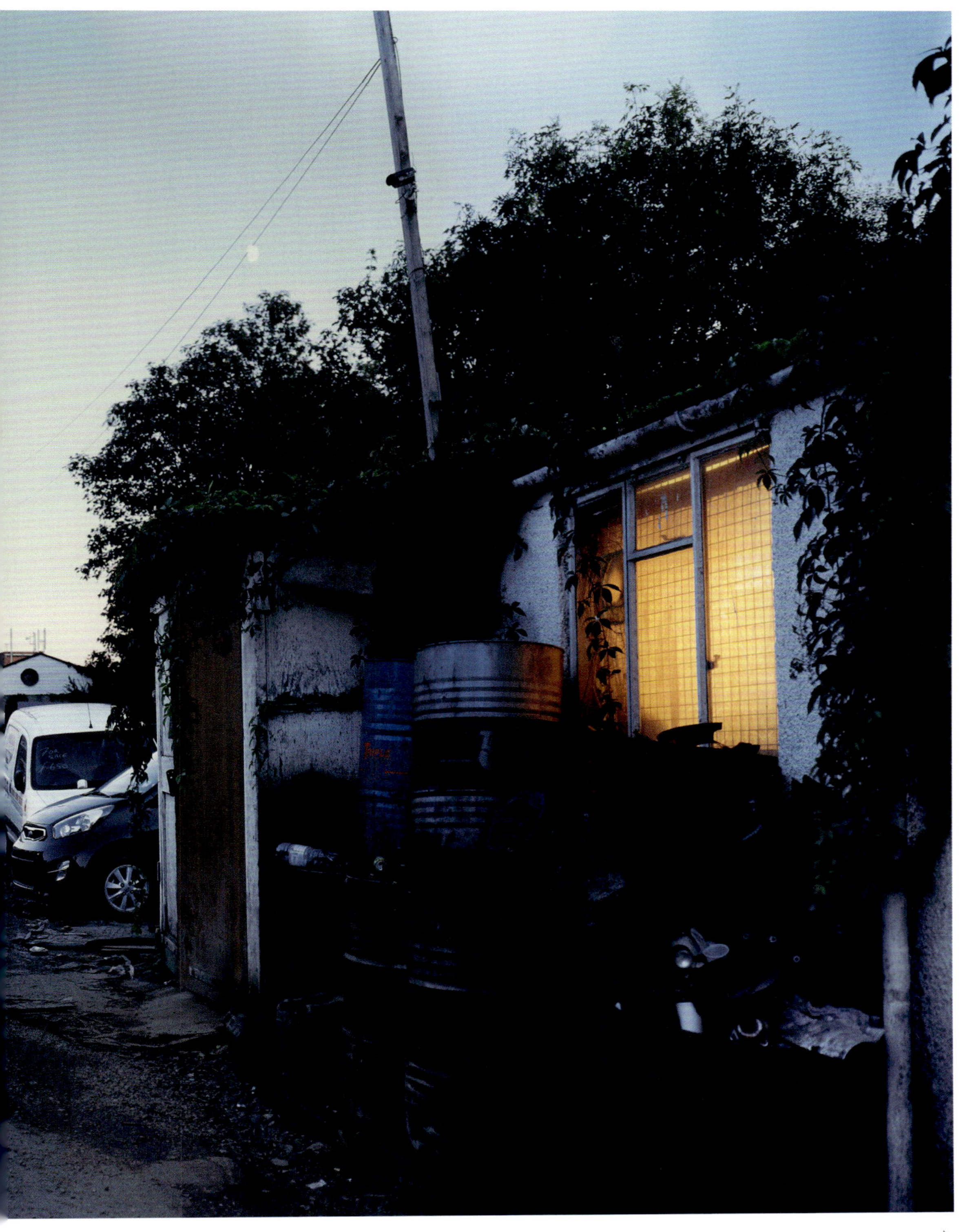

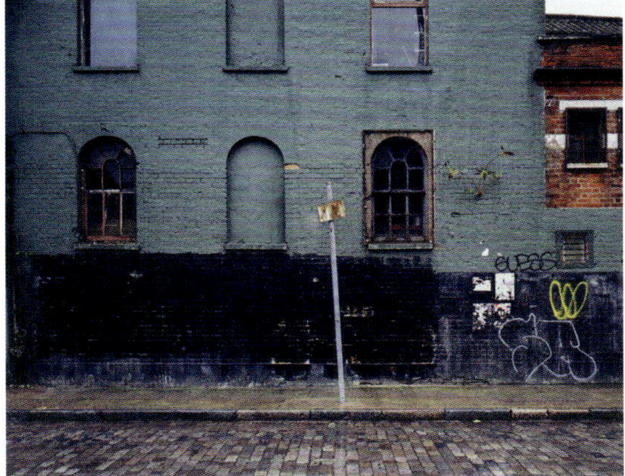

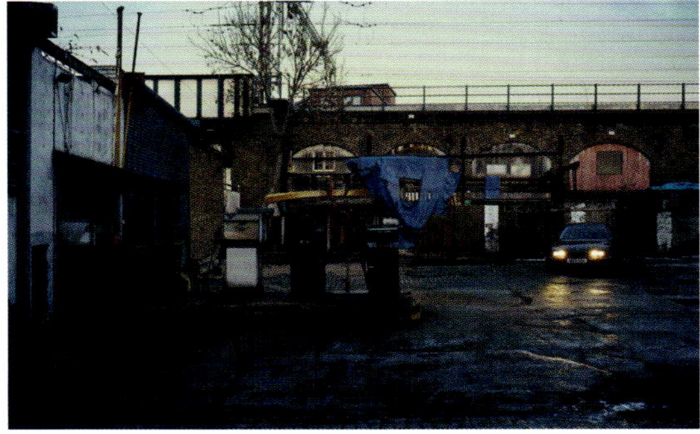

The stills presented here deviate from all the above approaches. Inspired by and related to my feature film, *Gholam* (2018), the work uses the real locations of the film, yet focuses on the 'rejected' cast, or the extras. Or they depict empty landscapes, with an implication of narrative. In this respect the images also differ from the usual film stills which often portray one or more characters, and are rarely devoid of people.

Set in London, *Gholam* tells the story of an enigmatic Iranian taxi driver, who doesn't like to talk about his past, doesn't care about his future, and doesn't commit to anything. A man with no past, no future, no 'convictions', he still gets involved in the conflict of a total stranger and carries it through, regardless of the consequences. The story contains an element of danger. The stills here, however, with their pared-down aesthetic, neither exhort nor prognosticate; neither show, nor name, the danger or the drama. Instead, the work presents a collection of enigmatic images, which leaves the narrative open to interpretation – telling the story differently or even inducing the anti-story! But, as in the film, they portray a unique image of London, the 'unseen' city of migrants, living on the edge – and the sense of being on the 'other-side'.

Throughout the film, the main character remains an enigma. So in these stills, he is not replaced or represented by any of the rejected cast, a strategy used to maintain or enhance the mystery, echoing the film. The only indication is his whereabouts; the places he's passed through or is heading to – or the hidden danger awaiting in these deserted landscapes, alluding to what is 'out-of-the- frame'.

Mitra Tabrizian, 2018

'That which is within the frame (characters, props) is a relatively closed system, and can be treated as a spatial composition. However, it can never be completely closed, because of the way it can define the "out-of-the-frame".'
Gilles Deleuze

Film stills are often photographs of the main character(s) taken on or off the set of a movie to introduce/publicise the film. The main purpose of such publicity stills is to help promote the film and stars. Shots can be taken during the filming or separately posed. Many of these have self-explanatory designations: seasonal gag shots, fashion stills, commercial tie-ups, poster art, clinch shots (special posing for print advertising) and candid snapshots. By far the most popular of these many kinds of film stills are those portraying glamour, menace or gag interpretations.

Pages 73–77
Mitra Tabrizian
Film Stills
2017–2018

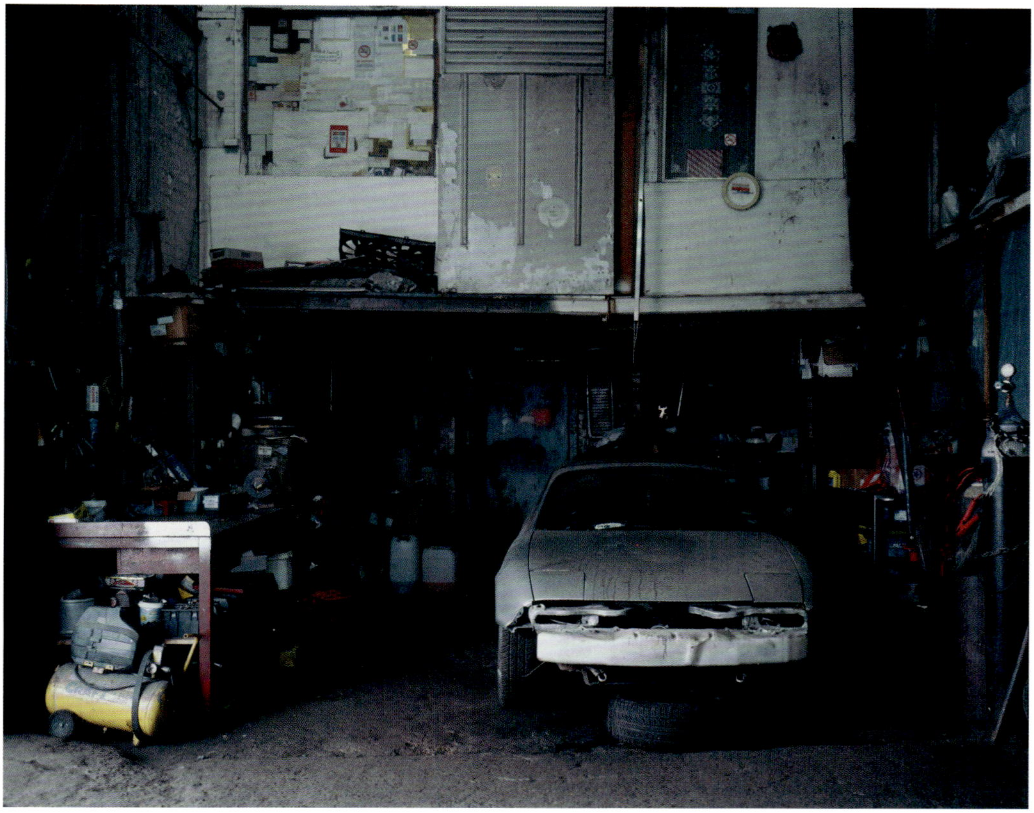

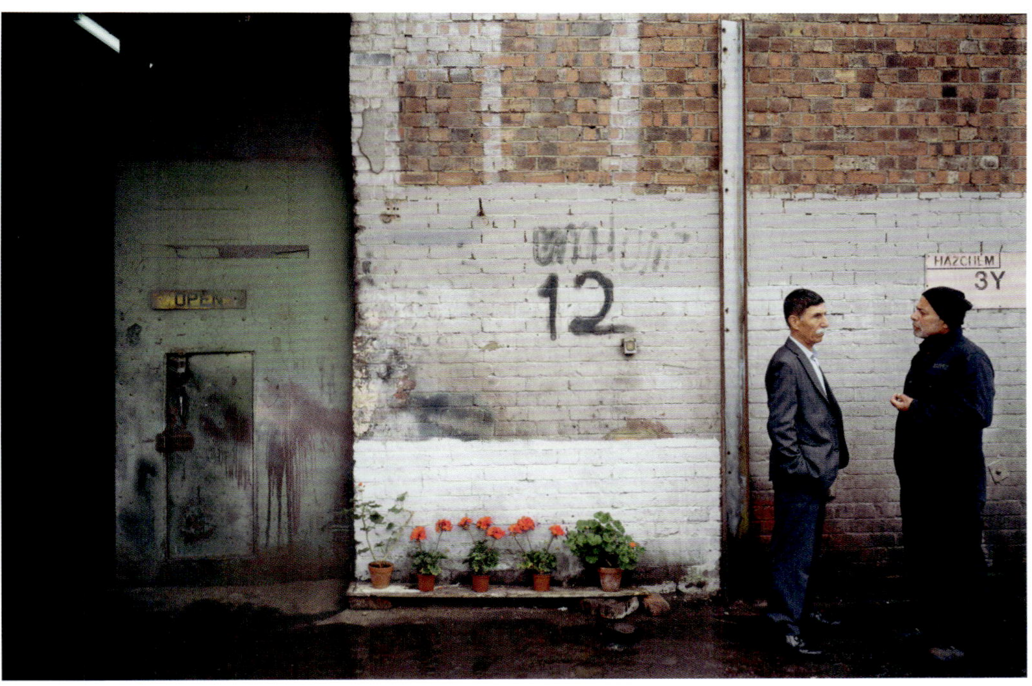

Mark Wallinger

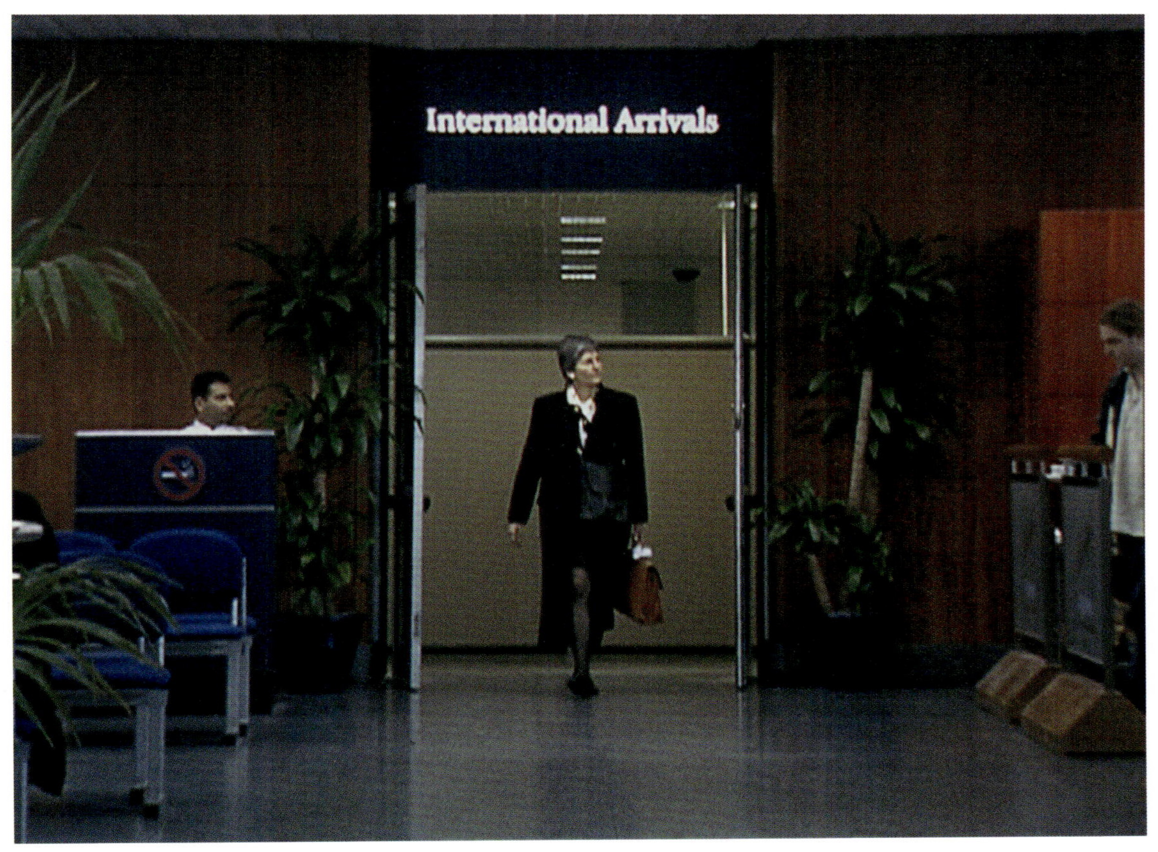
International Arrivals

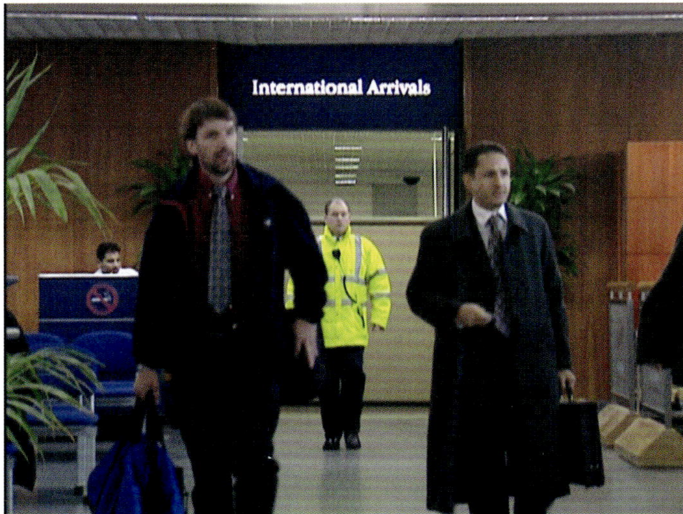

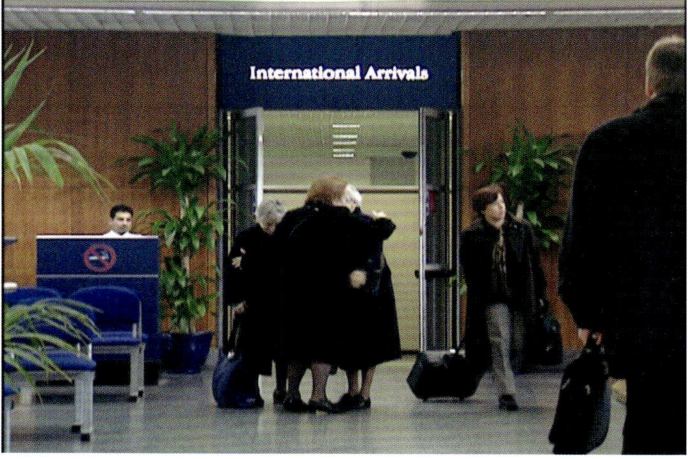

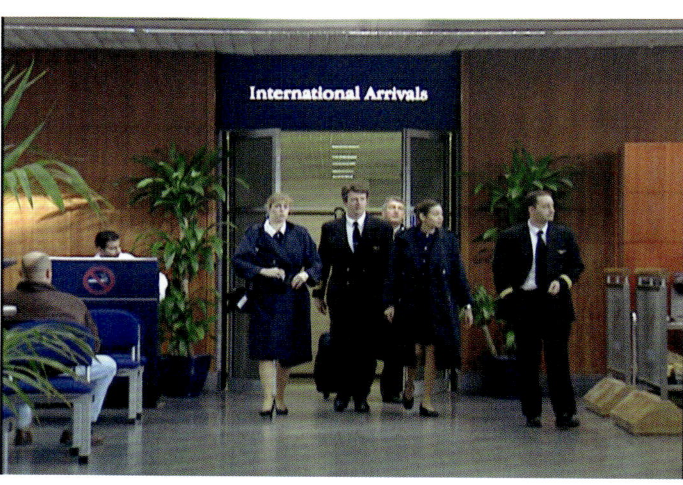

Pages 79–81
Mark Wallinger
Threshold to the Kingdom   2000

In negotiating the more or less authoritarian or coercive apparatus of the state which define and control one's progress from 'air-side' to land-side', one is perhaps reminded of a secular equivalent of the progression from confession to absolution. Eventually, all that separates us from the no-man's-land and the official terra firma of the state are a pair of automatic doors.

While earlier works such as *Angel* (1997) explored the rich symbolism available in negotiating our way around the city, this film plays with the symbolism that signals a change in state. The aura of security, the self-consciousness this induces and the little drama of the final gates opening are amplified and transformed by the soundtrack into an altered state or delivery into the Kingdom of Heaven itself. All roads lead to Rome. The ideal or vanishing point.

Allegri's *Miserere*, a setting of the fifty-first psalm, has been sung in the Sistine Chapel for centuries and the music was a closely guarded secret until Mozart, visiting as a fourteen-year-old, made a notation from memory.

Mark Wallinger, 2000

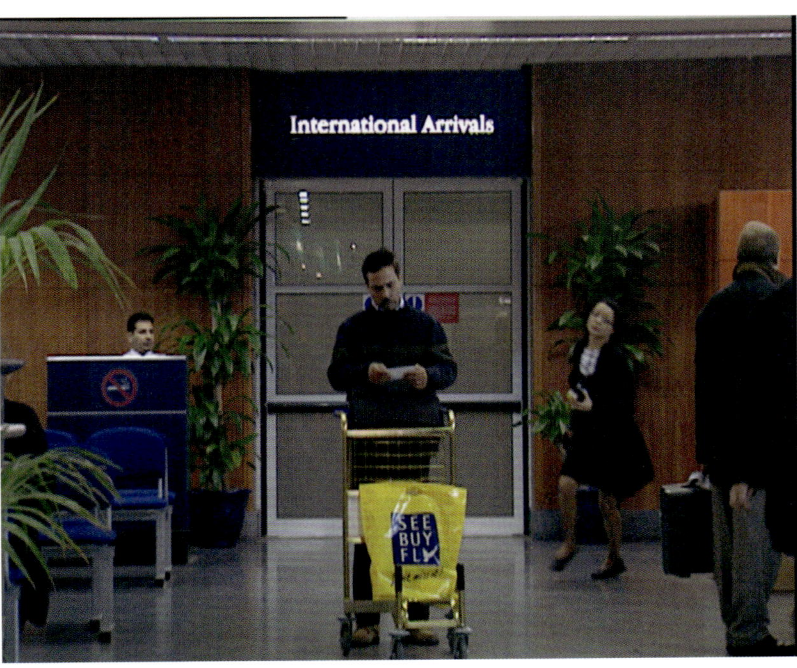

Osman Yousefzada

Osman Yousefzada

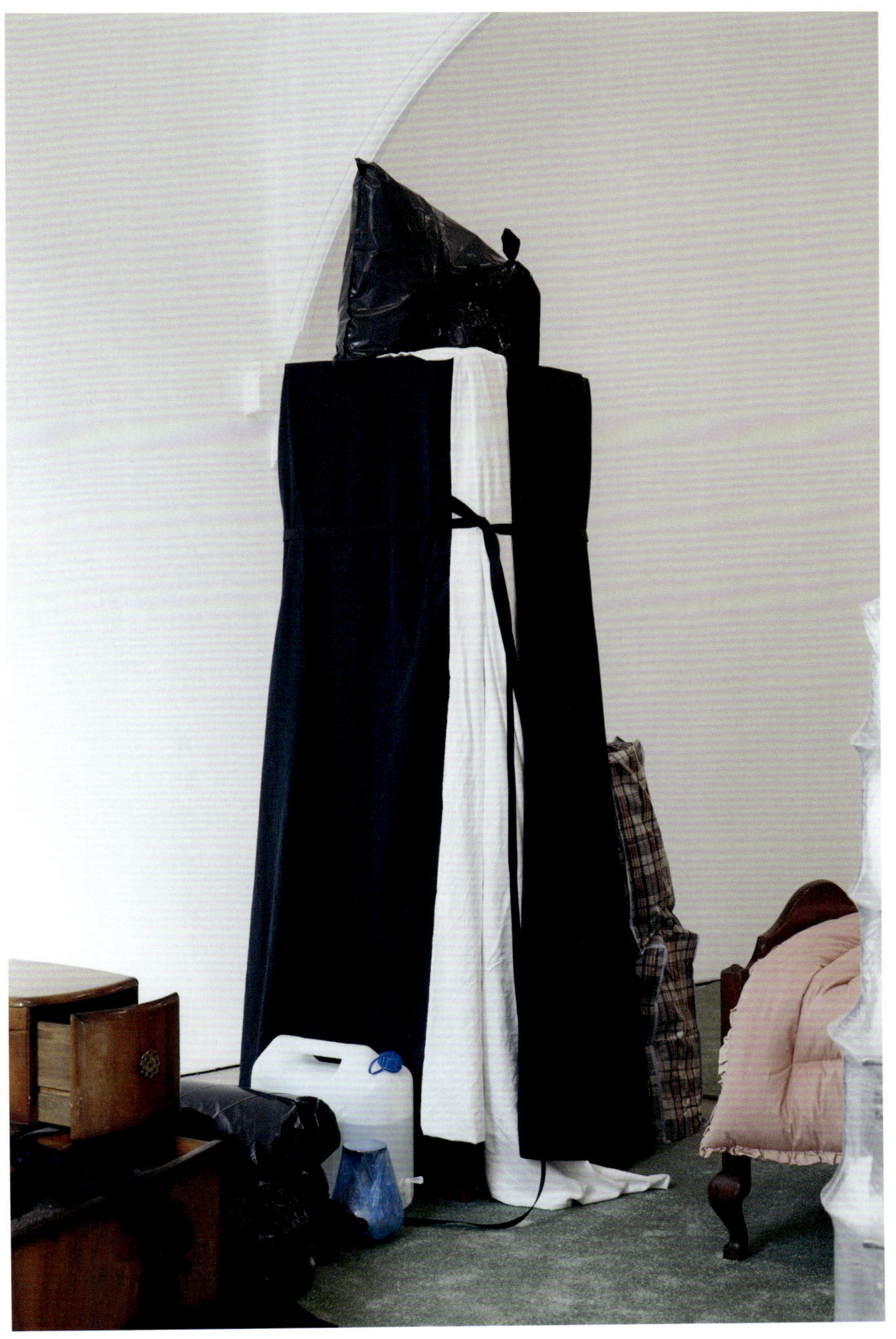

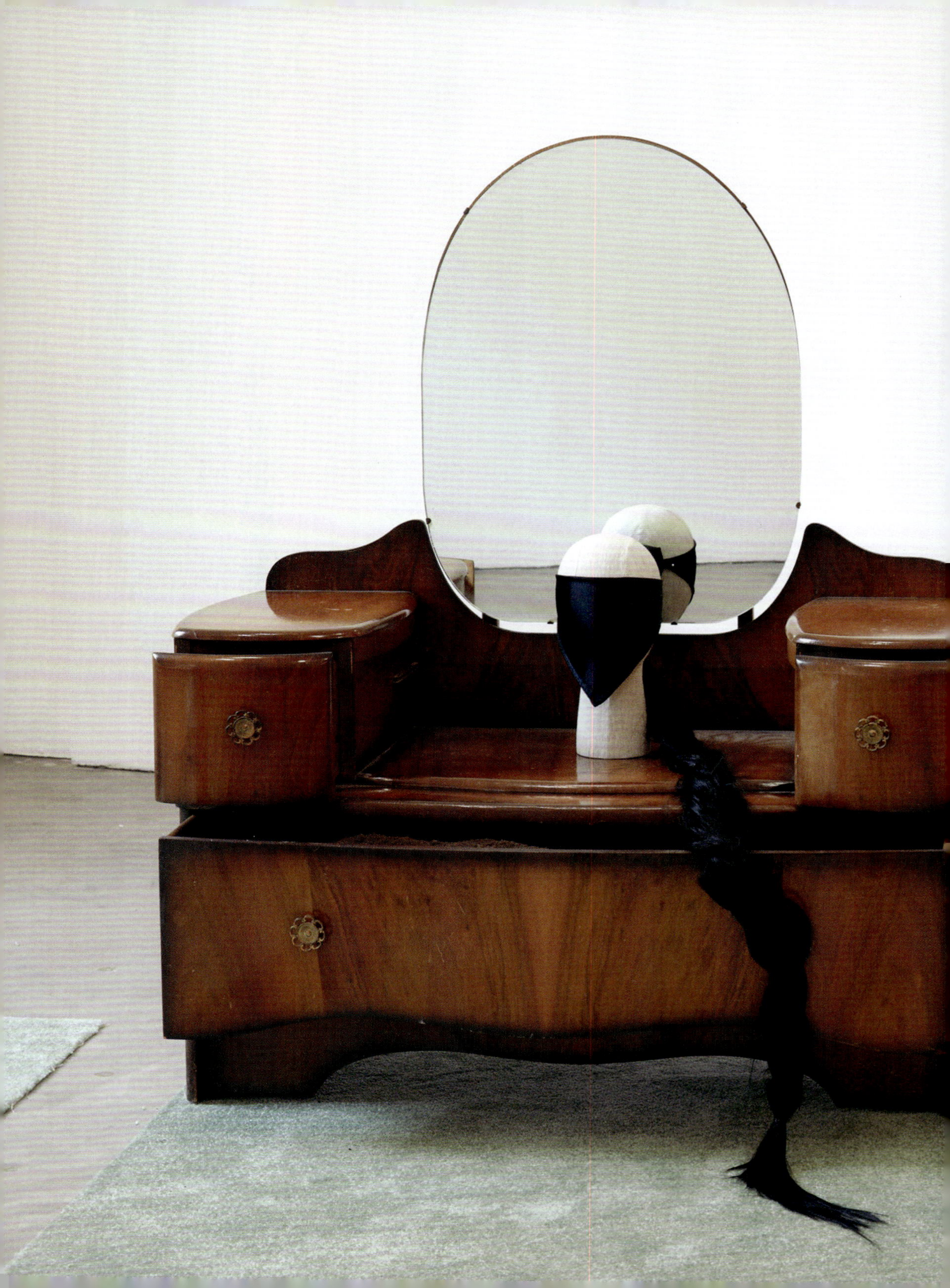

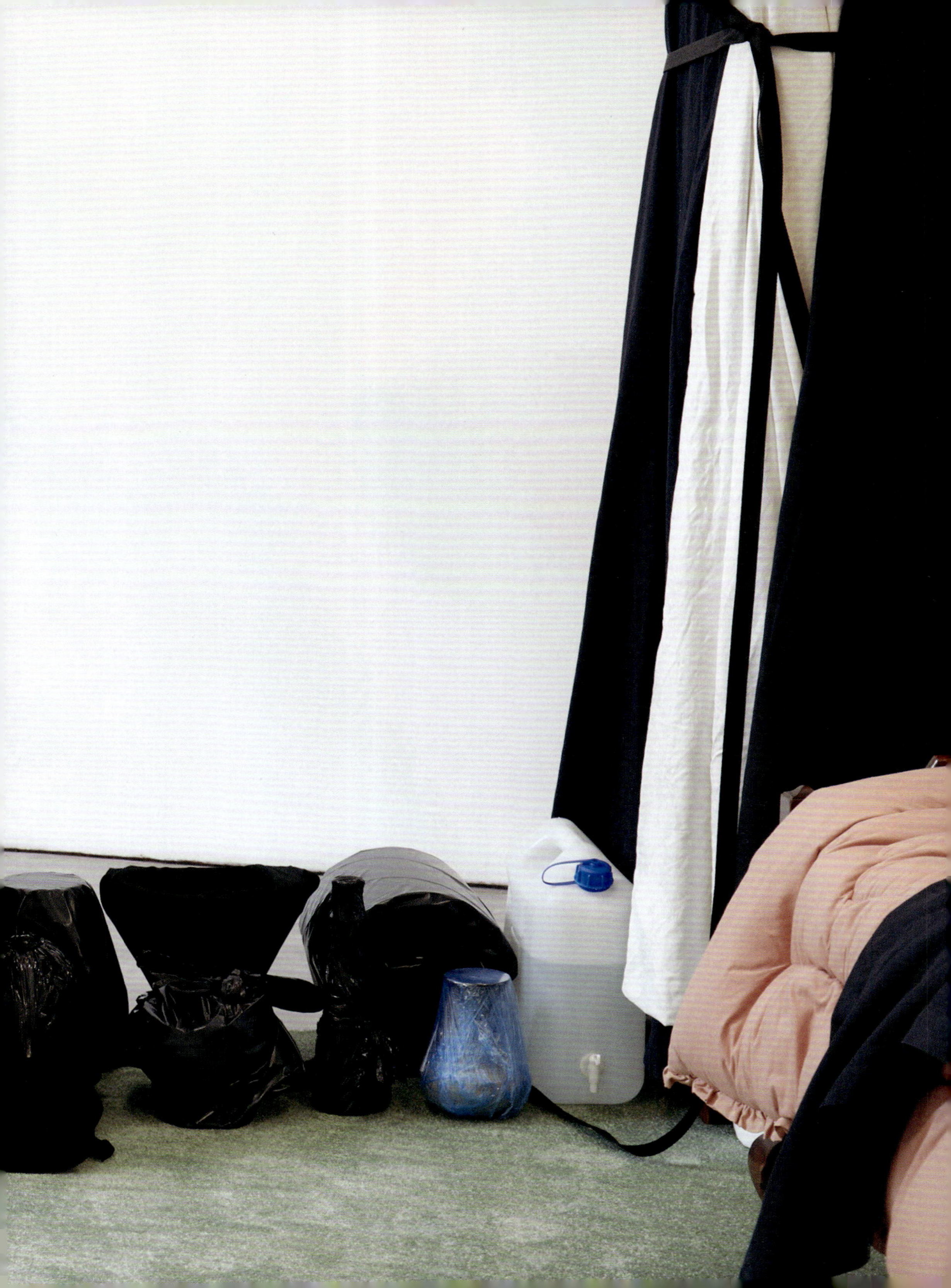

Pages 83–87
Osman Yousefzada
An Immigrant's Room of Her Own   2018

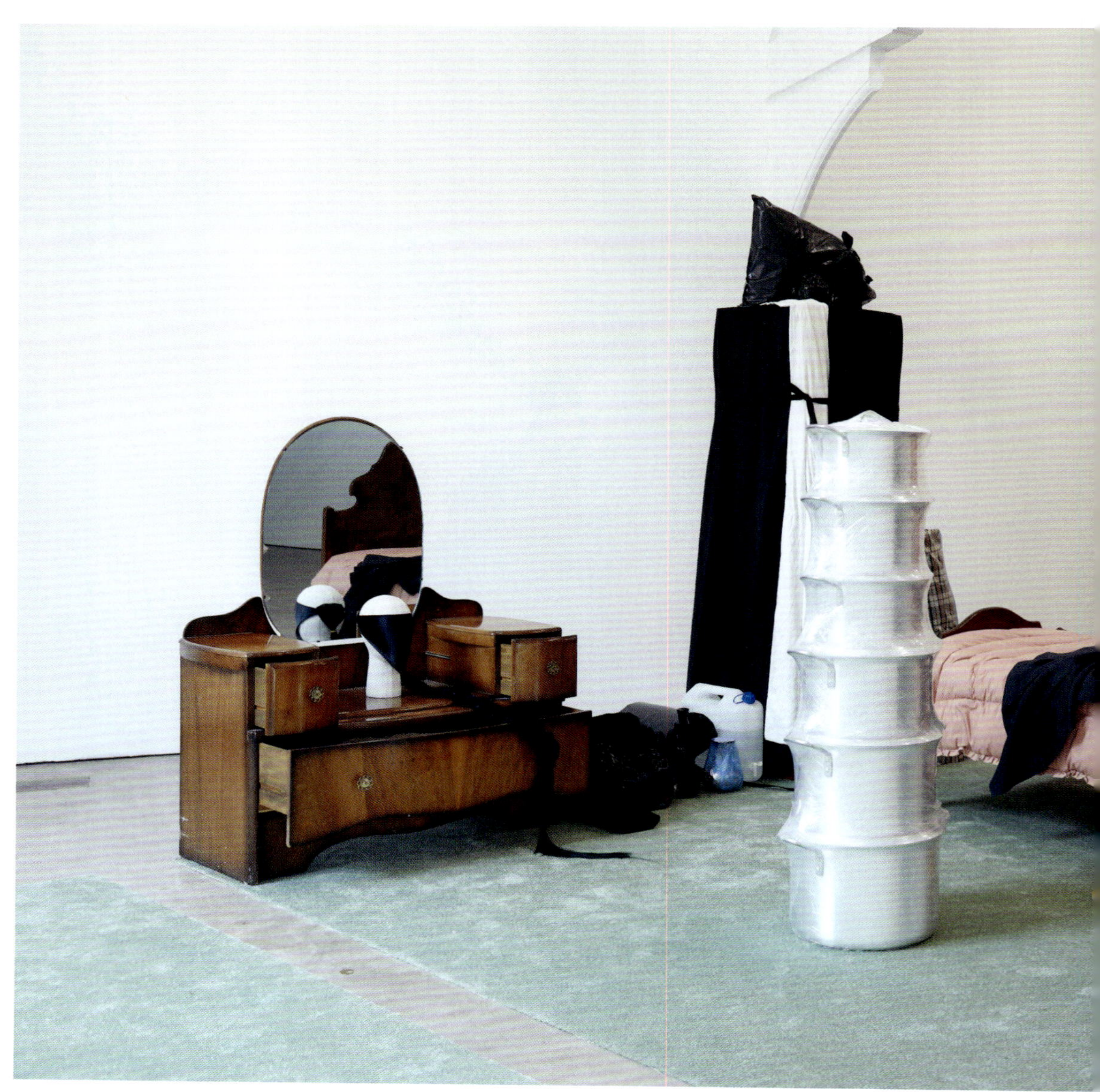

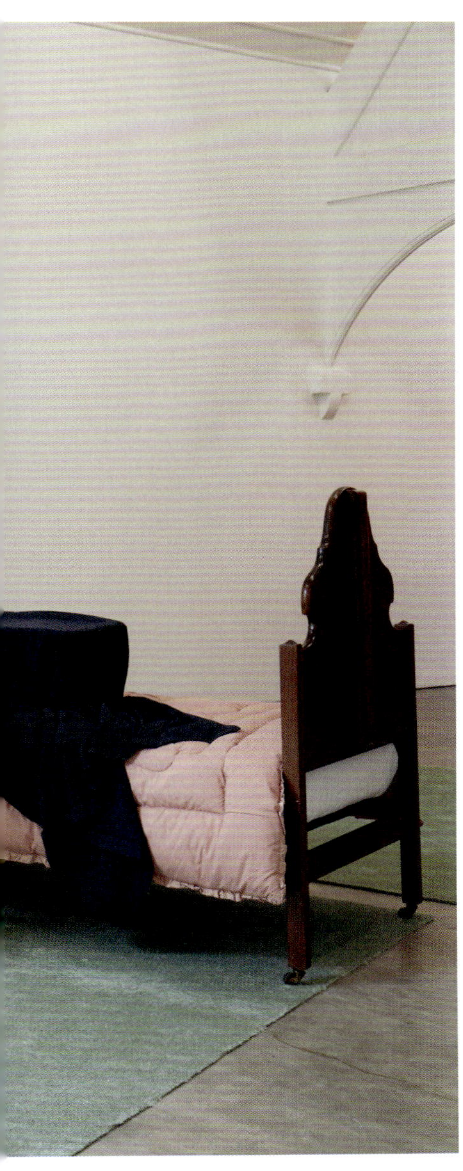

It was around this time that the life I knew as an active participant in the world of women was cut short. My existence there became taboo. The walls had grown taller, and the curtains thicker, and I couldn't peer over or around. Mum noticed I was getting older. I was nearly twelve. Time for me, as a young man, to stop hanging around the women in her salon, time for me to stop visiting them with Mum, time for me to stop playing with my sisters.

I had been ejected from where the joy and the colour came from. Now I would have to peer from behind the curtain and see who was around before I could go in. This light-violet damask curtain divided manliness on one side from the concealed colours of femininity on the other. The women's world was only a few feet away yet was no longer a space I could walk through with much ease. I was allowed near Mum, near close family and very close family friends, but it was never the same. Even if Hooriya Jaan was in the salon, Mum's best friend who had bathed me as a toddler and changed my nappies, I couldn't go in and speak or laugh with her if there were other women around. I had come of age, the worlds became segregated, and I could only reminisce as the distance between the male and female worlds grew bigger and bigger.

Osman Yousefzada, *The Go-Between: A Portrait of Growing Up Between Different Worlds*, Canongate Books, London, 2022

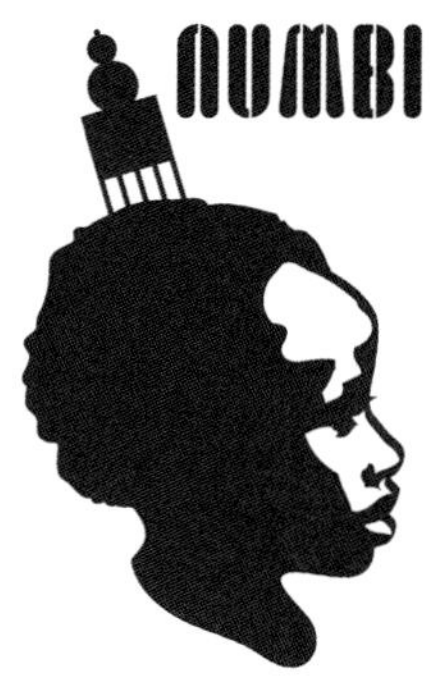

The Somali Museum:

A Conversation with Kinsi Abdulleh

Kinsi Abdulleh is an interdisciplinary artist and co-director of Numbi Arts, a Somali-led, African-centred culture and heritage organisation. Kinsi has worked in East London for over thirty years and her practice centres on people whose voices are suppressed or ignored, both within their own communities and in wider society. Numbi Arts' latest project is the Somali Museum, which underwent a successful crowdfunding campaign in Spring 2020, during the UK's first COVID-19 lockdown.

Numbi Arts and Whitechapel Gallery have a long history of collaboration; during a recent collaboration in 2021, we hosted a series of reading groups titled 'Postcards from the Diaspora', curated by Kinsi. The sessions were facilitated by Black womxn, non-binary and trans artists and thinkers, and focused on gender, decolonisation and agency.

This summer 2023, Kinsi presents the first exhibition of the Somali Museum at Whitechapel Gallery, sharing new work by artists who have been in conversation with the museum. Specially commissioned artworks will be gifted to the museum following the exhibition.

In this conversation, Kinsi discusses the issues and ideas that have informed this exhibition, including historic erasures of Black identities and the importance of preserving cultural memory for future generations.

Siobhán Forshaw, Curator: Community Programmes

You once said to me that the shortest distance between two people is a story. What are the stories that are important to the Somali Museum?

There are so many beautiful and inspiring stories in our communities that are untold or lost. In the absence of grand museums to house our stories, locating and sharing the importance of people is vital to us – we have always said it's not about collections, it's about collectives.

The most resourced national museums in the UK will often mislabel and inaccurately interpret the artefacts of Somali histories. Their archives are a space where colonial violence will be re-enacted, because we will always be wrongly understood, and offensive words will be used to describe us. Often, what will have been collected will be posed photographs of half-naked people, and you can imagine the violence of that – these are places collecting and displaying the teeth, heads and hair of human beings.

We want to intervene and centre human stories told in people's own words – to celebrate and share personal archives. For years I have taken oral histories and spent my time hearing directly from people. In particular, I want to platform the stories of women to redress imbalances in the ways men and women are described – you might have a great Somali mariner on the one hand and dismiss a woman's role as a housewife on the other.

It's a bit like land – if you don't claim and tell your own story, others will occupy that space and tell it for you.

Can you speak to what Numbi Arts is about and the kind of work you do?

At Numbi, we create spaces for community dialogue to happen, led by social justice and rooted in women's voices. Our work is collaborative, involving artists, writers, poets and musicians. We have been based in East London for the past thirty years, working in different community settings. The work that we do is Somali originated, but it's important to us that our work is inclusive of African diasporic voices. Our participants inhabit different identities and often their needs are not visible, so it falls to us to articulate those needs and provide that support. Our audiences are very mixed and the work we create is open to dreamers of all stripes.

Our origins are somewhat connected with the Whitechapel. Back in 2005, we put on a film festival and a series of public events with the Gallery. One of the films submitted was called *Numbi* by Fuad Abdulaziz, about a dance. It was a beautiful film, with a healing aspect. Two days before the festival was scheduled, the London bombings happened. The Gallery sits above Aldgate East station, where one of the bombs went off. It was terrible, you can imagine. But, despite this crisis, we went ahead with the festival and lots of local people came. With the collective that was formed through that festival, we decided to move forward together as Numbi.

You crowdfunded for the Somali Museum during the initial stages of the pandemic. What do you believe is the role of arts organisations during times of crisis, whether the bombing in 2005, the housing crisis in Tower Hamlets, or how the current conflict in Sudan reverberates within communities that you know and work with locally?

The thing is, crisis has never stopped and it's not going to stop. The reality is that this is the expression of the interconnected violence and exclusion that we in the global majority are subjected to. Until we admit the systemic oppression that is not by accident, we cannot address any issue in isolation.

It is terribly sad to hear the different ways that European conflicts are spoken about in the UK compared to African conflicts, which makes even clearer the hierarchy of whose lives are considered useful and important. Whilst I am never shocked by such language, it is dangerous and damaging to be exposed to it and, as a community, we deal with this every day.

I came to seek sanctuary in this country at the age of seventeen, to a country that starts and funds wars elsewhere and then creates a hostile environment for those who arrive on its shores, driven from their homes. My understanding through my own experiences is that amidst all of this, life goes on. And for some of us, art is a lifeline.

In this context, it is even more important to be prioritising and protecting the stories of our people and communities.

You have been co-director of Numbi for three decades. What does good and responsible stewardship of an arts organisation look and feel like to you, as a leader and as an artist?

We have a Somali saying – whoever holds the drum gets the most trouble. It's about a call and response. When you beat the drum, you are asking for a response. I have never viewed myself as a leader because seeking accolade and performative activism is not interesting to me. As an artist, I really do believe in social justice and this is the place that I move from – I think that if you are holding the drum, you are also accepting the responsibility. When you beat the drum, you have to be ready for a response – to hold ground. I choose to hold the drum, I do not choose to be a leader.

I believe that two-year-olds are great leaders – they are stubborn, they stand their ground, they will manifest what they want! The grown-up version of this is about giving service – whatever you are given, you need to pass on. If you have gained a position to nurture or make things happen, that is the rent you pay. In Numbi we make things happen collectively – though there might be one person who lights the match, I really do believe in doing things together.

The projects you run locally are often focused on nurturing young talent. What are the main challenges facing the young people in your life right now?

It is a very difficult time for young people. A lot of ours are struggling with instability, having lost their jobs. Many were confined to their family homes during the COVID-19 lockdowns, where they cannot be themselves or feel safe in their identity, and this is bad for their mental health. Access to support is much harder these days, and so we're finding that they have nowhere to go, physically or emotionally. The work we do provides relief from these situations – we create unconditional spaces to gather with people who give strength. I am always impressed by their resourcefulness and support for each other. Our hope is to recruit a core team of young people, to create secure employment and skills training which is desperately needed. Instead of always being workshop participants, we want to help them to become leaders.

Can you say more about the future plans for the Somali Museum and why it matters so much at this moment?

They say that when an old person dies, a library burns to the ground. We must archive the work that we have done for the past three decades, to ensure it is not lost – to give something to those who come after us. The Somali Museum will be a living museum, not one solely of objects. Somali people are one of the oldest Black communities in the UK and yet we don't have a single landmark or memorial, not a street name to acknowledge us. This is complete erasure. It is a denial of our human right to have our culture recognised and made accessible.

We don't have to rely on others giving us permission. We can create our own space; we can be independent. At the same time, we can't do it by ourselves and we don't want to! We need solidarity and support from the wider community to make it happen.

It takes huge energy to fight the different battles: within your own community that wants you to assimilate to a rigid view of what Somali culture is. Then you have a wider society that is blind by choice and treats us as one homogenous group. One of our other mottos at Numbi is *Get Free!* That's what the museum stands for; it is an invitation to our Somali communities to come together, shape the future and preserve what is important to us: through this self-determination we're trying to get free.

List of Exhibited Works

Rana Begum
No. 1272 Chainlink, 2023
powder-coated chainlink
Courtesy of the Artist and Kate MacGarry, London

William Cobbing
Written in Water, 2022
plywood, Perspex, Jesmonite

Sarah Dobai
The Donkey Field, 2021
2k video
19 mins 40 secs

Susan Hiller
Untitled, 1999
Five wrapped parcels (various sizes);
hand-written labels; vintage wooden
luggage trolley; looped audio
Courtesy of Lisson Gallery

Susan Hiller
The J. Street Project (Film), 2002–2005
Video installation, single channel projection
67 mins
Courtesy of Lisson Gallery

Susan Hiller
The J. Street Project (Index), 2002–2005
Wall-based installation: 303 archival colour
inkjets mounted on Kapaline, oak frames,
index and map in adhesive vinyl
Courtesy of Lisson Gallery

Jerome
Action Black, 2018–Present
oil, oil pastel, vinyl flooring
Dimensions variable

Matthew Krishanu
Bows and Arrows, 2018
oil on canvas
Courtesy of a Private Collection

Matthew Krishanu
Boy on a Climbing Frame, 2022
oil on canvas
Courtesy of the Artist and Niru Ratnam, London

Matthew Krishanu
Four Children (Verandah), 2022
oil on canvas
Courtesy of a Private Collection

Matthew Krishanu
In Sickness and In Health, 2007–2022

Girl on a Bed, 2007
acrylic on canvas
Courtesy of the Artist

Girl with Slippers, 2007–2012
acrylic on canvas
Courtesy of a Private Collection

The Wedding Dress, 2009
oil on linen
Courtesy of the Artist

Elephants, 2010
acrylic on linen
Courtesy of the Artist

Hospital Bed (Barts), 2021
acrylic on canvas
Courtesy of the Artist

Hospital Bed (Whipps Cross), 2021
acrylic on canvas
Courtesy of the Artist

Bedroom (Mother and Baby), 2022
acrylic on canvas
Courtesy of the Artist

Four Poster Bed, 2022
acrylic on canvas
Courtesy of a Private Collection

Hospice Bed, 2022
acrylic on canvas
Courtesy of the Artist

Home Bed (Feeding Tube), 2022
acrylic on board
Courtesy of the Artist

Home Bed (Mother and Child), 2022
acrylic on canvas
Courtesy of the Artist

The Convalescent (after Gwen John), 2022
acrylic on canvas
Courtesy of the Artist

Janette Parris
This is Not a Memoir, 2023
Eight digital drawings

John Smith
The Girl Chewing Gum, 1976
16mm film transferred to digital file
12 mins
Courtesy of the Artist, Kate MacGarry, London
and Tanya Leighton, Berlin and Los Angeles

John Smith
Citadel, 2020
HD Video
16 mins
Courtesy of the Artist, Kate MacGarry, London
and Tanya Leighton, Berlin and Los Angeles

Alia Syed
Fatima's Letter, 1992
16 mm film transferred to digital file
19 mins
Courtesy of the Artist and LUX, London

Mitra Tabrizian
Film Stills, 2017–2018
Nine C-type photographic prints
Special thanks to Alan Harris and Zadoc Nava

Mark Wallinger
Threshold to the Kingdom, 2000
projected video installation
11 mins 10 secs

Osman Yousefzada
An Immigrant's Room of Her Own, 2018
Installation

Credits

17–19
Rana Begum, *No.1225 Chainlink, Desert X*, 2022, Courtesy of Begum Studio, Photography by Lance Gerber

20–21
Rana Begum, *No.1242 Chainlink*, 2023, Courtesy Begum Studio, Photography by Philip White

23
William Cobbing, *Written in Water*, 2022, Courtesy of the Artist

24–27
William Cobbing, *Written in Water*, 2022, Installation view, Fish Island, London, Courtesy of the Artist

29
Sarah Dobai, *The Donkey Field*, Installation view, CAST, Cornwall, 2022, Courtesy of the Artist

29–31
Sarah Dobai, film stills from *The Donkey Field*, 2021, Courtesy of the Artist

33
Susan Hiller, *Untitled*, 1999, © Estate of Susan Hiller. Photography by Todd-White Art Photography

35
Susan Hiller, *Judenplan, Würzburg*, image 297 from *The J. Street Project (Index)*, 2002–2005, © The Estate of Susan Hiller. Courtesy Lisson Gallery

36–37
Susan Hiller, detail of *The J. Street Project (Index)*, 2002–2005, Wall-based installation © The Estate of Susan Hiller.
Photography by Todd-White Art Photography, Courtesy Lisson Gallery

38–39
Susan Hiller, film stills of *The J. Street Project (Film)*, 2002–2005, © The Estate of Susan Hiller. Courtesy Lisson Gallery

41
Jerome, *Pure*, Oil, Action Black, oil pastel on canvas, Courtesy of the Artist

42–43
Jerome, *Mayfly on Wheels*, Installation, Photography by Sae Yeoun Hwang

44
Protestors at Parliament Square, Photography by Sae Yeoun Hwang.
Mayfly on Wheels at Parliament Square decorated by protestors, Photography by Sae Yeoun Hwang

45
Jerome, detail of *Child I'm Home* Installation, Filet Space, London, Photography by Linghui Ng.
Close up of food served to public as part of *Child I'm Home* Installation at Filet Space, London, Photography by Linghui Ng

47
Matthew Krishanu, *Bows and Arrows*, 2018, Courtesy of a Private Collection, Photography by Peter Mallet

48
Matthew Krishanu, *Four Children (Verandah)*, 2022, Courtesy of a Private Collection, Photography by Peter Mallet

49
Matthew Krishanu, *Boy on a Climbing Frame*, 2022, Courtesy of the Artist and Niru Ratnam, London, Photography by Peter Mallet

50
Matthew Krishanu, *Hospital Bed (Barts)*, 2021, Courtesy of the Artist, Photography by Peter Mallet.
Matthew Krishanu, *Hospital Bed (Whipps Cross)*, 2021, Courtesy of the Artist, Photography by Peter Mallet

51
Matthew Krishanu, *The Convalescent (after Gwen John)*, 2022, Courtesy of the Artist, Photography by Peter Mallet

52
Matthew Krishanu, *Girl on a Bed*, 2007, Courtesy
of the Artist, Photography by Peter Mallet

53
Matthew Krishanu, *Four Poster Bed*, 2022,
Courtesy of a Private Collection, Photography
by Peter Mallet

55–57
Janette Parris, *This is Not a Memoir*, 2023, © Janette
Parris and Montez Press. Courtesy of the Artist

59–61
John Smith, film stills from *The Girl Chewing Gum*,
1976, Courtesy of the Artist, Kate MacGarry, London
and Tanya Leighton, Berlin and Los Angeles

62–65
John Smith, film stills from *Citadel*, 2020,
Courtesy of the Artist, Kate MacGarry, London
and Tanya Leighton, Berlin and Los Angeles

67–71
Alia Syed, film stills from *Fatima's Letter*, 1992,
Courtesy of the Artist and Lux, London

73–77
Mitra Tabrizian, *Film Stills*, 2017–2018, Courtesy
of the Artist

79–81
Mark Wallinger, film stills from *Threshold to the
Kingdom*, 2000, © Mark Wallinger. Courtesy of
the Artist

83–87
Osman Yousefzada, *An Immigrant's Room of Her
Own*, 2018, from the exhibition *Being Somewhere
Else*, Ikon Gallery, Birmingham, 2018. Installation
view. Image courtesy Ikon. Photography by
Stuart Whipps

Project Team

Gallery Technical Manager: Alejandro Ball

Development Administration Support: Christy Chan

Asymmetry Curatorial Fellow: Eugene Yiu Nam Cheung

Director's Assistant: Claudia Contu

Curator: Family Programme: Helen Davison

Audiences and Communications Officer: Colette Downing

Curator: Community Programmes: Siobhán Forshaw

Head of Visitor Services and Civic Engagement:
Luke Gregory-Jones

Development Manager, Grants and Foundations:
Jacqueline Kent

Director of Audiences and Communications: Jenny Lea

Curator: Schools and Teachers: Kirsty Lowry

Director of Education and Public Programmes:
Richard Martin

Director of Development: Rummana Naqvi

Curator: Youth Programmes: Amelia Oakley

Head of Exhibitions (Interim): Helen Sainsbury

Curator: Public Programmes: Jane Scarth

Curator: Special Projects: Katrina Schwarz

Head of Publications: Evie Tarr

Director: Gilane Tawadros

Visitor Services Supervisor: Beatrice Taylor-Searle

Senior Development Events Manager: Alice Thomson

Technical Production Manager: Sam Williams

Published to accompany the programme:

Life Is More Important Than Art

Whitechapel Gallery, London
June–September 2023

The season is generously supported by:
Sir Frank Bowling
The Life Is More Important Than Art Exhibition Circle

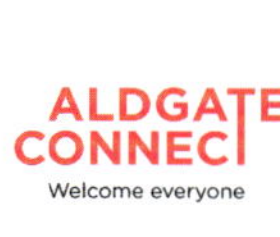
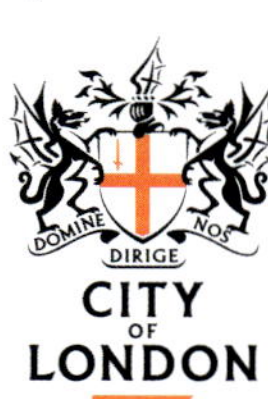
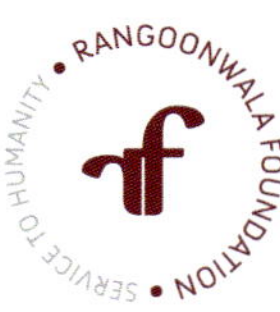

Curators: Gilane Tawadros and Janette Parris with
Katrina Schwarz
Editors: Gilane Tawadros and Katrina Schwarz
Head of Publications: Evie Tarr

Designed by: Herman Lelie
Layouts by: Stefania Bonelli
Repro: Dexter Pre-Media
Printed by: Gomer Press, Wales, UK

First published in 2023 by Whitechapel Gallery, London
© 2023 Whitechapel Gallery

All rights reserved. No part of this book may be reproduced
or transmitted in any form or by any means, electronic or
mechanical, including photocopying, recording or any other
information storage or retrieval system, without prior
permission in writing from the publisher.

The publisher gratefully acknowledges the permission granted
to reproduce the copyright material in this book. Every effort
has been made to trace copyright holders and to obtain their
permission for the use of copyright material. The publisher
apologises for any errors or omissions and would be grateful
if notified of any corrections that should be incorporated in
future reprints or editions of this book.

A catalogue record for this book is available from the
British Library.

Whitechapel Gallery
77–82 Whitechapel High Street
London, E1 7QX
whitechapelgallery.org

Distributed outside the United States
and Canada by
Thames & Hudson
181A High Holborn
London, WC1V 7QX
Tel: +44 (0)20 7845 5000
sales@thameshudson.co.uk

Printed on the underside of the cover: Janette
Parris, detail of 'Ilford Palais', *This is Not a Memoir*,
2023, courtesy of the Artist and Montez Press

Pages 6–7: Susan Hiller, detail of *The J. Street
Project (Index)*, 2002–2005 © The Estate of
Susan Hiller, courtesy of Lisson Gallery
Photo by Todd-White Art Photography

ISBN: 978-0-85488-319-6

Whitechapel Gallery